MEMORIES OF THE
CULTURAL REVOLUTION

MEMORIES
OF THE CULTURAL
REVOLUTION

POEMS

By Luo Ying

Translated by Denis Mair

UNIVERSITY OF OKLAHOMA PRESS : NORMAN

Library of Congress Cataloging-in-Publication Data

Luo, Ying, 1956– author.
  [Wen ge ji yi. English]
  Memories of the Cultural Revolution : poems / by Luo Ying. — First
edition.
    pages cm
  ISBN 978-0-8061-4917-2 (pbk. : alk. paper)
  1. China—History—Cultural Revolution, 1966–1976—Poetry. I. Mair,
Denis C., translator. II. Title.
  PL2880.U834W4614 2016
  895.11'52—dc23

                            2015023714

The paper in this book meets the guidelines for permanence and durability of
the Committee on Production Guidelines for Book Longevity of the Council
on Library Resources, Inc. ⊖

1 2 3 4 5 6 7 8 9 10

CONTENTS

 # PREFATORY POEM

Night . . . I rise and listen for that sound from afar
When it passes . . . those hooves or feet pump with calm determination
Day and night . . . it trails me . . . glares at me . . . sets itself against me
Without shape . . . exuding foul odor . . . a loud cough making it shudder
Crimson tongue coiling around souls or the limbs of skeletons
It never flies, yet its huge wings won't stop flapping
It forces me to run in shadows . . . to hiss like a cornered snake
When viewed as just another incarnation . . . everything turns quiet
Its gasps become a sea of wretched sighs heaved by old men next door
Past events . . . unbearable to recall those ends unraveling in silence
Terror and abjection like poisoned water . . . blocking the world's
     passageways
You imagine all is torn . . . then a streak of dawn appears
Blush of pink . . . lacking substance . . . extending without edge
It even waves huge arms and greets the land like a Master of History
It spits out sharp teeth in derision of our bygone century
Thus I disdain vistas of sky and sun . . . even moon and stars
Looking up, I hurl a curse into the cosmos—"What a fucked-up time!"

18:32, October 5, 2012. Seat 6A on Flight MU5171 from Huangshan to Beijing.

 TRANSLATOR'S NOTE

The "Great Proletarian Cultural Revolution" (1966–1976) was a defining phase of China's stumbling course into modernity, and because of China's size, it is an important page in world history as well. It was a time characterized by politicization of daily life, ultra-leftist mass movements, and factional struggle. To understand what is happening in China today, we need to know how the aftereffects of that era continue to play out in society. Luo Ying immerses us in the period with his short poetic narratives of decisive moments. His poems skillfully combine youthful experience with broader perspectives gained in retrospect. He also narrates episodes from the subsequent era of rapid economic growth, showing how the lingering effects of the Cultural Revolution continue to pose difficult issues for people in their careers and personal lives. Luo Ying's position as an eminent businessman gives him a special window through which to observe broad currents in Chinese society. While preparing to write this book, the poet organized an oral history project and conference in his home province of Ningxia, demonstrating his serious commitment to historical reflection and reconciliation. In the pages that follow, a young individual's inner life bears witness to a period when ideology threatened individuality. In spite of the terrible things that happened, this collection of poems proves that society did not lose its power to foster unique individual voices.

Luo Ying is a true believer in poetry, because poetry is what saved him. When he was thirteen, a teacher sent one of his poems to the biggest newspaper in Ningxia. Seeing himself in print gave him an avenue to prove himself beyond the scrimmage of street life. His commitment to poetry was further strengthened when the *Ningxia Daily* recommended him for admittance as a special-entry student to Peking University just after the Cultural Revolution. Although he went on to pursue a career in business, his grounding in humanistic studies is a strong undercurrent in his thinking. As a Forbes-listed CEO, he has been a generous donor to humanities programs at his home university and elsewhere.

As translator, I have focused on rendering Luo Ying's work rather than on tracing its sources. However, the reader may be interested in knowing where this collection fits into poetry schools and movements within

China. Luo Ying graduated from Peking University in 1980, so he can be counted as a member of the "Peking University School" of poetry. In terms of youthful influences, this means that he was mentored by Xie Mian, who was the first eminent scholar to endorse the home-grown symbolist movement called Misty Poetry. Thus he would naturally have been affected by late 1970s enthusiasm for the Misty Poets that swept China's campuses. But more than that, he was immersed in the sources from which Misty Poetry sprang. These included the poetry of Tagore, Pushkin, Whitman, and Baudelaire. They also included works by the Tang-era masters and Qu Yuan's romantic "vision quest" poems from China's classical era. Added to Luo's personal mix were works by pioneering modernists of the 1920s and 1930s—Xu Zhimo, Bian Zhilin, and Guo Moruo—and more recent poets of leftist romanticism, such as Ai Qing, of the 1950s and 1960s. Nazim Hikmet's work was translated from Turkish during the 1970s and was read enthusiastically by Peking University students. Another strong influence was the work of Pablo Neruda. As a young man, Luo Ying was reading translations of Neruda fresh from the pen of the premier translator of Latin American poets, Zhao Zhenjiang, who was a professor at the university.

Luo Ying was able to combine these sources into a strongly individual voice for two reasons. Firstly, he had a strong appetite for theoretically rigorous works by Sartre, Foucault, Heidegger, and Tsungkhapa. These thinkers gave him perspectives from which to view the broader background of his lyrical impulses. Secondly, he consistently engaged in real-world activities—as a business executive, mountaineer, and philanthropist— giving him experiential grist and pragmatic balance that he could channel into his poetry writing.

Like other eminent poets from Peking University such as Xi Chuan and Zang Di, Luo Ying's oeuvre shows wide range, beginning with personal reflection and lyricism (*Notes of an Urban Vagabond*), then venturing into philosophical series such as the existential "Bunnies," as well as conceptually structured works such as *Ninth Night*, a book-length series of animal mono- logues. After arriving at maturity as a poet, he left his Misty Poetry sources and even his Peking University School roots behind. In recent years he has engaged in a succession of projects that explore various kinds of concep- tual terrain. *Death · Image* is a series of meditations on human mortality; *Water · Sprite* is an extended series focusing on the "lightness of being" and dedicated to the "God of Small Things"; *Memories of the Cultural Revolution* is a narrative series that reflects on an era's legacy; *Ninth Night* grapples with the emotional, internal consequences of a life lived at the forefront of China's economic development; *7 + 2 Mountain Climber's Journal* is a contemplative record of his climbing adventures; *Green Tara* enacts Buddhist themes of impermanence and compassion on a stream-of-consciousness level. All of these projects share a common aim of using poetry as an avenue of exploration. Even his most external narratives show the mind in the process of summing up history and experience. Even his most inward reflections gain traction from his grounding in real-world involvements.

In order to remain active as a poet, Luo Ying has learned to juggle his business activities with intervals of creative time. For him, making time to write is part of his art. When he can put aside business affairs, he gives himself fully and passionately to the concerns of a poet, but then he must quickly pull himself back into the world of boardroom meetings and business trips. His acts of writing must be kept within a clear temporal frame. For this reason, he ends each poem with a notation of time, place, and circumstance: this is a reflection of his temporally mindful poetic practice.

Denis Mair
December 2014, Beijing

MEMORIES OF THE CULTURAL REVOLUTION

BARE BONES THAT WERE MY FATHER

1.

You could hardly call my father a kind man
Once, with a glare and a shout, he slapped me when I was two
He held me while I cried, lying on the brick bed
He watched me out of the corner of his eye and listened for my sleeping
    breath
When I was three, he was trussed with thick ropes and hauled off
They said he was a counterrevolutionary, caught in the act
He was a revolutionary prize of the "Ningxia Two Antis Campaign"[1]
An enemy of the people, he was held at Xihu Prison Farm
Because of too many enemies in one cell, Father fell ill
He stashed three months of medicine, then gulped it all down
When they buried him in the dunes, his eyes were still staring
His eyebrows were still bushy, his lips still thick
An enemy got no gravestone, so he rotted like a nameless dog
Just a heap of bones in the wasteland, no color or smell
Later the revolution achieved new victories; he was absolved for 3,000 yuan
But I still don't know how to rescue his soul from those cords that tightly
    bind it

    18:50, October 5, 2012. Seat 6A on Flight MU5171 from Huangshan to Beijing.

---

1. In the early 1960s, a movement to "strike down the local nationality-based, anti-party clique" and "strike down evildoers and outlaws," known as Shuangfan Yundong ("The Two Antis Movement"), took place in Ningxia.

2.

Memories of my homeland begin with hunger and abject poverty
But memories of my father end with his being arrested in public
Those revolutionaries rounded up a lot of counterrevolutionaries
With rough hemp cords they bound my father's wrists and throat
My father tried to yell, "I'm a Party member, loyal to Chairman Mao"
At the time, I wrongly thought those stifled sounds were pleas
Those tight ropes must have cut him to the heart; his eyes were closed
Then he meekly lowered his head like an obedient soldier
As a colonel in the Northwest Guerilla Corps, he had surely killed KMT
    troops
He defeated Old Chiang, then got busy along the northwest frontier
He transported grain to Lanzhou, built roads and bridges in Ningxia
He became secretary, took the lead, dreamed up plans for the Party
He was arrested in the name of revolution—of course
People shouted and slapped him, wouldn't let me cry or stamp my feet
He wouldn't open his eyes to see the terrified child before him
He trembled slightly when he heard the bellows of his old "fighting buddies"
One of Mao's soldiers, he would do as the Party said, go where he was needed
He knelt in a truck bed; in a blink he was gone in the darkness

19:21, October 5, 2012. On airport loop to Terminal 2 at Beijing Airport.

3.

My dead father was a restless soul with no grave to call home
Maybe due to his cruel treatment of enemies when he fought Old Chiang
He must have thrust a bayonet deep into an enemy's chest
Maybe just a peasant from his district, wearing a new uniform
When Father gulped those pills, they say he didn't make a sound
He rolled on the floor, holding his chest tightly
The wardens dragged him by the legs like a dog, but he didn't kick
That must have been his way of showing loyalty
In twenty minutes, they covered him in one of the desolate graves
Countless graves were dug and ready for counterrevolutionaries
When the revolution needed a fighter, Father was that fighter
When the revolution needed a sacrificial victim, he was that victim
He vanished from the world in a chilling way
By a brutal procedure; the grief was left to his family
He died like a dog, and I had to live like a dog . . .
I would never kill myself, but I would never have a new life
I would pay the highest respects to every grave plaque
I would honor every white bone with the name Father

22:46, October 5, 2012. Changhe-wan in Beijing.

4.

Father cut himself off from the people; twenty years later, he came back as
    3,000 yuan
There was even a certificate: "Comrade Huang Junfu has been absolved."
My share was 500 yuan, which paid for three days of drinking
I told my classmates he had gotten rich in Hades by selling his soul
But I kept seeing my father's eyes in my liquor glass
He was shimmering as if seen through tears
In an era when everything was absolved, I became a drunk
Thanks to Father, I had money for liquor; I could wear a respectable face
On Helan Mountain we four siblings gave our parents a joint grave
We wrote Father's name on paper and put it in the grave
We also carved his name with Mother's on the plaque
His name in big red lacquer characters gazed out at us
I didn't have the courage to don a soldier's cap and salute him
Because he might have felt anger toward his "fighting buddies"
If he were alive, I think he'd grab a gun and line them up against a wall
He didn't know that times would get worse, even more unspeakable
After that, I liked to drink liquor and spout off—play the big talker
I always told my female classmates that my father had been a colonel

23:24, October 5, 2012. Changhe-wan in Beijing.

MY MOTHER, WHO WAS LAME

1.

I think my illiterate mother only recognized a few characters
She would beat me with a duster, her eyes gleaming with malice
Now I think she must have been playing her husband's role
Being a counter-rev's wife put her lowest among women
She had four children and hoped they would all go to school
Each day she dug up dirt and sold it, never raising her head
By faint starlight, she pulled her wooden cart out the gate
A woman in her thirties, harnessed like a mule
As she made her way along the street, insults followed her
It seemed she never bathed or put on new clothes
Her steps were rushed, as if she were walking down a byway of apocalypse
She looked grim-faced and careworn while cooking or washing
Maybe because we lacked clothes and rations, with no one to borrow from
Maybe she worried how her children would live if she died
I saw her wailing and pounding the ground with her fists
She would say, "Why doesn't the government do something?"
When she passed, kids on the street mimicked her wails and stomping
When she passed, neighbors along the street pursed their lips in contempt

20:55, October 15, 2012. Changhe-wan in Beijing.

2.

Mother went to fetch his corpse; by then it was just a ghost of the dunes
She walked among the barren graves, looking for his remains
There were new untended graves—too many to count or visit
Mother bowed before all the graves, calling her husband's name
On the street she wailed and sobbed at everyone
People drew back, saying, "Serves you right—counterrevolutionary's wife"
She sat silently under a streetlight late into the night
Her unfed children lay curled on the brick bed against the wall
From then on, she would rise at night and walk aimlessly
When she fetched water, she would often make a wrong turn
She dug up dirt and sold it to support her children
Shamelessly she scavenged cabbage leaves and bone scraps
While she was digging dirt at daybreak, the city wall collapsed on her
Luckily a manure picker found her hand protruding from the dirt
At least she didn't die, but she was lame in one leg from then on
At least she could work, despite the big scar on her head
So the kids in our little city would mimic her limping
So the adults in our city grinned to see her gashed scalp

21:21, October 15, 2012. Changhe-wan in Beijing.

3.

I can't remember a time when Mother was good-tempered
In a sudden rage, she would beat me until I shook with fright
When I won a fight with a neighbor kid, she thrashed me
When a neighbor kid cut open my head, she kicked me in the belly
She chased me the three miles to school for the bun I had squirreled away
    in my bag
At shaming sessions for no-goodnik children, she made us admit our faults
If my head wasn't bowed, she would shout, "Hit him! Hit him!"
I held back tears; she often swallowed tears in those revolutionary years
Later I would climb onto the roof, to read and daydream out of reach
She would leave the door unlatched so I could sneak into bed at night
When she rode off to work, I would run behind her bike
If I stumbled and fell, she would not look back
If I scarfed up melon rinds and old peach pits, she didn't care
She never shed tears, but I could see that her eyes were red-rimmed
Once she even spent five cents on a mung bean cake for me
That cake had a heavenly taste I will never forget
Once while I was scrambling for food, my foot went into the stove
She held me for days, and I will never forget that tenderness

21:52, October 15, 2012. Changhe-wan in Beijing.

4.

Mother did die in the end, from breathing propane while on night duty
She was fifty, born in the Tiger Year; her life energy was used up
I had been sent to a farm and could feed myself, so I guess it was her time
Now I think she must have hated the raw deal she got in life
She lay suffering from bedsores, couldn't bring up phlegm
My cries made tears trickle from her eyes, which filled me with joy
For eight months she fought for life, then one day she stopped breathing
The lame woman with a scarred head wore new clothes in her coffin
Though she was still a counterrevolutionary's wife, there would be no more
    petitioning in Beijing
I wouldn't be beaten anymore, though I was still a counterrevolutionary's son
We buried her at Helan Mountain and still sweep the grave each year
At least she has a gravestone carved with her name, Yan Xiuying
We buried Father's name with her, pretending they are buried together
It occurs to me that we never heard her mention his name
After I got rich, I had their grave rebuilt with large stones
It is a high mound now, where I think she will be glad to live
She can feel safe in this world now that her man has been absolved
Her son is a man of wealth and substance; his name is on the Forbes list
This year I will do prostrations before her grave
I will honor her with that great, pitiful title—"Chinese woman"

22:16, October 5, 2012. Changhe-wan in Beijing.

OIL WORKER HUANG YUBAO

Huang Yubao is an oil worker; of course, he is also my brother
As for the bitterness he tasted as First Son, he never mentions it
He left school to learn a trade, painted flashy posters at a theater
The comics he brought home opened my eyes to literature
With paint-smeared clothes, he worked long hours in our little city
One day he brought home a potato that his kind boss had given him
He gave me most of it; I gulped it down and howled for more
He glared and pushed me away, then stormed out the door
To earn more money, he worked in the Gobi oilfield
He often said it was an honor to be an oil worker
As a counterrevolutionary's son, he went through struggle sessions
After the sessions, they made him paint giant Mao portraits on walls
At ten I went through a session with him, then we walked home laughing
We sang revolutionary songs, loud and badly off key
On sand dunes we caught crickets and voles, chased after rabbits
After dinner we would sort ration coupons into piles
Coworkers would force a smile and walk by at a distance
Because he could kick pebbles into the air with his work boot

22:52, October 16, 2012. Changhe-wan in Beijing.

HUANG YUYING, THE SURVEYOR

My big sister, Huang Yuying, was quick-tempered and sharp-tongued
I think she went to an oilfield after junior high, then to nursing school
To keep my sobs from bringing bad luck, she stuffed my mouth with salt
After fights with Mother, she wanted to hang herself or crash into a tree
Later she became a surveyor, spent months in wild mountain country
Once she watched three coworkers get swept away by a flood
Maybe because she was a girl, she didn't matter enough to be shamed in a
 struggle session
Maybe it was her tirades that made people cringe and grit their teeth
In class warfare, her shrewish disposition was a big advantage
People felt scared and fed up, yet wanted to stay on her good side
That was a crazy time, and you never knew what someone might do
Luckily those capitalist roaders and power holders had been toppled
They no longer dared to arrest and kill in the name of revolution
With her charade of wanting to smash everything, my sister got ahead in life
After we buried our mother, she had her hands full raising her children
When I went to college, she would occasionally send me 30 yuan
Now she often calls to ask if I want some of her sauce made from deep-fried
 chilis

23:15, October 16, 2012. Changhe-wan in Beijing.

GEOLOGY TEAM MEMBER HUANG YUDI

Second brother Huang Yudi was my antagonist
As boys, driven by hunger, we often fought over food
He held back when he hit me, but I used all my strength
We went to steal soybeans from a horse trough, and he ran off and left me
Instead of beating me, the groom gave me bean cake and played with me
One time, after he fell off a wall, his bruised lip swelled alarmingly
A neighbor boy would attack us both, but we dared not hit back
Because the boy's father stood there with his hands on his hips
After high school, my brother did geology surveys, trekked over rough terrain
I don't think he ever sent me money, and he rarely smiled at me
He went to the Commerce Bureau, was made head honcho of appliance
    purchasing
I'll bet he took kickbacks; he never lacked for tobacco and liquor from clients
With our different views on the Cultural Revolution, we quarreled endlessly
He was a Rebel, I was a Royalist—both holding the Red Book high
We couldn't remember our father's face, never called upon his memory
In our quarrels with Mother, we both disrespected her
We were half-tamed wolves, with bared teeth and boorish manners
Now he holds a post under me, but I sent him home to retire

23:35, October 16, 2012. Changhe-wan in Beijing.

MY NAME IS HUANG YUPING

1.

Actually, my childhood name was Huang Gaping
Facing starvation in 1960, Mother wanted to give me away
My sister wailed and held me tight; she wouldn't let me go
I lived through that, but the road ahead was not smooth
Due to my constant crying, my family called me "God of Ill Fortune"
Due to my frequent bedwetting, my rump was swollen from their beatings
At dawn Mother went to haul dirt, leaving two potatoes on the stove
Second Brother often got up first and gulped them down
When I was pushed out of bed in my sleep, I couldn't climb back on
Eating wild jujubes made my shit come out red
For picking cabbages after harvest, Brother and I were locked in a farmer's pen
Sister shouted and wailed until nightfall for our release
In the winter months, I got chilblains and sniveled endlessly
I wiped my nose on sleeves that were as hard as armor
In primary school, I was the prime suspect in classroom thieveries
If anything went missing, the teacher would inspect my bag
When my classmates pounded marching drums, I hid tears of envy
My heart felt the pangs of never wearing a red scarf

23:51, October 16, 2012. Changhe-wan in Beijing.

2.

Those days as I recall them were full of insults
I stole corn, swiped ducks, and smashed people's windows
I was too small; our cruel neighbor would beat me black and blue
I was a tenacious fighter; I threw a brick through his window one night
A newborn baby almost got hit in the head, causing a big scare
The neighbors called a truce and gave me brown sugar candy
In those wolfish days, you got what you tore off with indomitable teeth
I was a scoundrel and a scamp; to the revolutionaries, I was a hoodlum
Begging for food in mess halls, I would gulp down unfinished soup
In Yinchuan Park, I fought with vultures for butcher scraps
Once I mistook a turd for a pretzel and gulped it down
I learned that eating excrement was not the end of the world
I learned that I was only a renegade in our great motherland
I learned that I could roam for three days unfed without dropping dead
I knew not to wolf down others' leavings, for fear of puking them up
I can testify that melons stolen by moonlight are extra delicious
Like a cockroach of the nation, I was despised but not exterminated

20:36, October 17, 2012. Changhe-wan in Beijing.

3.

I haven't met the Grim Reaper, yet he has brushed past me many times
I should have been eaten by wolves or buried alive; I should have died from
    a fall
At the age of eleven, I climbed Helan Mountain, heard wolves howl outside
    an empty temple
I kept them at bay all night, throwing stones with quivering arms
The fury of that long night is still enough to scorch my heart
At work in a production brigade, there were no wolves, so I shot dogs
At fourteen I laid open a ruffian's head with a brass belt buckle
His uncle nabbed me and marched me to a riverbank
He dug a pit and made me jump in, ready to bury me alive
I looked him in the eye and cursed his forebears for eighteen generations
He sighed and drove off without another look
I walked until daybreak and collapsed in front of our house
In autumn, picking apricots on Helan Mountain, I fell on some rocks
A shepherd carried me home and had me drink his child's urine
I believe it brought me back to life; I got home lying in a gravel truck
I leaned against the wall in a daze, unable to eat or drink
When I got rich, I went for a physical; my hepatic vein had long since been
    severed
The Grim Reaper must have gotten drunk; that day he was sleeping it off

21:03, October 17, 2012. Changhe-wan in Beijing.

4.

My mother was a child bride; she ran away from Huangyuan in Qinghai
I was a fatherless boy; later I was a hellion who liked to flirt with death
My mother was cornered for three days by wolves, but they let her go
I lived as a renegade in my motherland; there was nowhere to hide
The workers' team came to restore order, showing erections as they fawned
 over the female students
They viewed me with contempt, told me to disavow my
 counterrevolutionary dad
The army came to teach discipline, made me step forward and cheer for
 Chairman Mao
They told me to confess all the filthy thoughts deep in my soul . . .
Qiu Zhongfen headed the army; his wife was top leader at our school
She never looked me in the eye, always wanted to have me expelled
She put me on indefinite detention; the black marks would stay in my folder
I called her "Fileface Qiu" and smashed the office window in front of her
A girl of good background called me a hoodlum; I poured an inkpot down
 her blouse
A classmate made fun of my mother; I knocked his front teeth out right
 there in class
I played hooky and read *Resurrection* on the city wall, feeling glad to be human
Reading *Spartacus* convinced me I was a gladiator's descendant
The Count of Monte Cristo made me hatch plans of lifelong revenge
I was one of the *Humiliated and Insulted*, with every right to hurl curses

21:50, October 17, 2012. Changhe-wan in Beijing.

5.

I can't recall how many struggle sessions I endured in my youth
But I recall that I never bowed my head
One classmate guarded me with a wooden gun; he was urged to hit me
As I came down from the platform, I bashed his head with a stool
I can't recall all the times I was beaten in my youth
But I know I never begged for mercy
When I caught one of the culprits alone, I lashed him with a steel whip
While a ruffian was swimming, I shot an air-gun pellet at his face
There were no wolves in our little city, but my soul was torn by teeth
The sun was bright in our frontier city, but that never warmed my heart
This is a story that makes you forlorn in the telling
Those were years that people are sad to recall
That period of history is humiliating even to mention
That was an ordeal that left scars on our nation
We killed our own fathers, shamed our own children
Today, beneath our fine attire, we hide the pain in our hearts
The barren graves have been swallowed up in Gobi's dunes
Let us be done with them, those harsh and heartbreaking years

22:34, October 17, 2012. Changhe-wan in Beijing.

CHAIRMAN MAO'S LITTLE RED GUARDS

At ten I was already a little red guard, a fighter for Chairman Mao
The Chairman Mao badge I got was pinned to my chest night and day
We broke all the windows at our school as a sign of revolution
We ordered teachers to clean the toilets, made them hang their heads and
    confess
We pasted up maxims, shouted slogans, maintained revolutionary order
Only sparrows dared fly over our little-red-guard heads
My calligraphy came in handy—I could write big-character posters
Critiquing the principal for too much homework and classical
    memorization
In front of Chairman Mao, we accused the head teacher for making us sit still
And for standing us in a corner and drumming on our heads with chalk
One day I ordered the principal to cough up 10 yuan for armbands
Then as rebels we took over the school seal and authorization letters
First thing in the morning, we paid allegiance to our beloved leader
We ordered the phys ed teacher to recite Chairman Mao quotes
In the end our old principal hanged himself from a locust tree in shame
We chanted slogans, claimed he had "cut himself off from the people"

09:13, November 6, 2012. 1416 Wembley Road, San Marino, Los Angeles.

THE LITTLE RED BOOK

The Red Book contained quotes from Chairman Mao, in gleaming red and
    gold
Holding it high, we stoked our fighting spirit, bent on destroying the old world
In debates we quoted the supreme directives; their meaning had to be
    brought to life
The aim was to knock down capitalist roaders, then stomp them with our feet
With the Red Book in hand each day, our eyes would often brim with tears
Each line by the Chairman was supreme truth, each word gave off gold light
They charted our unerring course toward revolution, with a red glow in
    our hearts
We harried landlords and critiqued monsters, raging without mercy
We stretched out the principal's arms like an airplane's wings, paraded him
    with a plaque and dunce cap
Before the Red Book, he turned pale and closed his eyes
He asked to recite the quotations loudly to show his loyalty
He hoped to get the book back, to turn over a new leaf
But when he hanged himself, the book was flung into the mud
Now I think it was because of his pent-up resentment
The half-wet, half-blackened Red Book was discovered near his body
The next day, still furious, we held a session to critique his ghost

06:47, November 7, 2012. 1416 Wembley Road, San Marino, Los Angeles.

THE DRILL-TEAM DANCE

The drill-team dance was for waging revolution deep within the soul
We danced it during parades, danced it at debates, even danced it at home
Fists against chests, heads thrown back, staring off into the distance
Now it makes me think of Vajra deities standing guard at temple doors
Its simple, forceful moves were good any time of the day, for any age or sex
Fat, thin, tall, short, fat cats or eggheads—it moved our Worker-Peasant-
    Soldier feet
When *Long live Chairman Mao* rang out, we would freeze in a group pose
Dressed in army fatigues and army belts, sporting glittery Mao badges
The old principal was spotted before dawn, secretly practicing the moves
We called out his stooping hangdog posture as an affront to Chairman Mao
At the shaming session against him, we danced drill and sang Mao songs
The sun high in the heavens made our blood seethe, *Long live Chairman
    Mao!*
The drill-team dance was a spiritual outlet for my revolutionary will
At each sunrise, that grand melody arose in my heart—"The East Is Red"
Gazing into the distance, I noticed that my fists were balled up tightly
In my heart rose intentions fierce enough to smash the world to smithereens

07:25, November 7, 2012. 1416 Wembley Road, San Marino, Los Angeles.

21

THE MANGO

Beloved Chairman Mao sent a golden mango as a gift to the Rebel Faction
Heavens! People in our frontier city waited for three days, unable to sleep
    at night
They beat drums and gongs, did the drill-team dance, emptied lanes to line
    the streets
Faces shone with tears and full hearts stretched near breaking . . . *Long live*
    Chairman Mao
The Rebel Faction held the mango high, striding like emissaries of God
Some said golden rays went up to the clouds; fragrance filled the city
Being small, I was pushed aside and didn't see what the mango looked like
Maybe due to my background, I didn't count as one of the Chairman's
    preferred fighters
The mango's arrival kindled our city, whipping revolution fever to new heights
The city shouted, "Carry out the Cultural Revolution, even if we are
    reduced to dust"
No one knew whether the mango rotted away or if someone got his teeth
    into it
People switched from civil assault to martial defense, and bloodlust took over
The street where the mango passed was a battleground where gunshots
    rang out
Dirges for the dead became our city's daily musical background
Later, due to eating many mangoes, I lost my revolutionary passion
Later, due to eating many mangoes, a dirge kept ringing in my ears

07:51, November 7, 2012. 1416 Wembley Road, San Marino, Los Angeles.

THE SUPREME DIRECTIVE

I miss the days when speakers across the city played the broadcasts from
 Beijing
We stood at attention, listening to the supreme directive from the Statehouse
Time and again, the Great Helmsman set our course through fogs of
 indirection
With the Red Book and a steel whip in hand, we stood ready to smash
 anything and everything
Having knocked down capitalist roaders, the next step was all-out fighting
We fought peers and teachers, to see who was most loyal to Mao
The speakers overhead played revolutionary songs and Mao quotes
Because they broadcast the supreme directives, we revered those speakers
Because dictatorship of the proletariat had to happen by seizing power
The speakers always transmitted the great message of the Great Leader
Knives were often flashed at rivals, but no one dared cut speaker wires
In a hail of bullets, no one thought to shoot at a loudspeaker
Many times I wanted to climb up and polish a speaker until it shone
I wanted Chairman Mao to know I was the most loyal little red guard
A multitude of crows perched on the speakers, their heads close together
People looked up at them, but none dared say they were bad omens

08:18, November 7, 2012. 1416 Wembley Road, San Marino, Los Angeles.

BIG-CHARACTER POSTERS

How fortunate I was to know calligraphy, to be able to write big-character
    posters
I was lucky to live during Cult-Revo, when I could let my voice ring out
Boiling bags of flour into paste, we were like soldiers on a battlefield
Pasting up posters along the street, we were like soldiers wielding bayonets
We could revile anyone and reveal private details about his family line
So crowds would form around the posters—reading aloud and by flashlight
Adversaries would respond with longer posters and even fiercer attacks
So our days in that city were filled with passion; there was always something
    to shock us
But once a fighter omitted a word in Chairman Mao's name
In the fervor of struggle, he even got the page order reversed
He was grabbed and given a public shaming, with no regard for factions
Someone poured paste on his head; they wrote all over his face
Some lashed him with steel whips until he writhed on the ground
Others spat in his face; in agony he shouted, *Long live Chairman Mao!*
That night the whole city turned out to read posters by flashlight
Some laughed coldly; some felt chills down their spines, wanting to cry

16:22, November 8, 2012. 1416 Wembley Road, San Marino, Los Angeles.

FORGING TIES WITH THE MASSES

In the days when we were all red guards, we all went forth to forge ties
Red guards toting bags and canteens squeezed onto trains for Beijing or
    Yan'an
They sowed the seeds of revolution, brought back scriptures of rebellion
Mixing sexes, baring arms, holding flags—they spread a red wave over the
    land
Capitalists needed shaming, and monsters still needed a good stomping
We went forth to forge ties, setting youth afire, goading China like a breed bull
I miss those days when we'd set out without money or extra clothes
Red guards roamed, ate, and fought across China, staying at reception sites
And yet my trip to forge ties in Beijing was a disaster
I squeezed onto a train, but was chased off later that night
A little red guard could not curse or fight, which put me at the lowest level
I wandered around a small station, watching Beijing-bound trains go by
I imagined the red guards at Tiananmen, getting to see the Great Leader wave
My temper flared; with Red Book waving, I cried and howled and made a
    scene
The stationmaster had a heart-to-heart talk with me, expounding on the
    revolution
"It's a long road to revolution, Little Comrade; Chairman Mao will be waiting"

17:06, November 7, 2012. 1416 Wembley Road, San Marino, Los Angeles.

HARRYING A LANDLORD

The little red guards were ripe for the fray—it was time to enter a village
  and harry landlords
This was a run-down, sparsely populated village along the Yellow River
It was winter; villagers in padded jackets brought out a lean old man
There was no sun; frowning villagers smoked and squatted at the edge of a
  field
A frequent struggle victim, he slumped and stooped, arms locked, face blank
His children peeked out from under a willow; they had a quilt of some kind
  with them
As little red guards, it was our glorious mission to harry landlords and
  capitalists
We took turns blaming him for all the wrongs of Liu Wencai and Huang
  Shiren[1]
He admitted it all, asked forgiveness, and offered two sheep and six chickens
He said the land reformers had gotten their figures wrong, put him in the
  wrong group
This made us mad—we knew our class enemy was cunning, the struggle
  complex
Someone knocked the old landlord down, kicked his head until he writhed
Ma Xiaohong—a perfect shrew at age eleven—tore at his face with her
  fingers
With all the strength of my ten-year-old arms, I pummeled him in the gut
He stopped making sounds; we headed home in ranks, singing Mao
  quotations
Next day I saw the landlord's children bearing a coffin, burning paper money

03:50, November 9, 2012. 1416 Wembley Road, San Marino, Los Angeles.

---

1. Liu Wencai 刘文彩 and Huang Shiren 黄世仁 were archetypal evil landlords, often referred
to as negative examples in propaganda campaigns. In 1965 a documentary titled *Shouzu-yuan*
(The Rent-Collecting Prison), about Liu's cruelty toward peasants, was made by Central Televi-
sion, and a museum with statues depicting Liu's cruel acts was set up in Dayi County, Sichuan.
Later a 1999 book, *Liu Wencai zhenxiang* (The Truth about Liu Wencai), by Xiaoshu Xiansheng,
argued that most of the negative evidence was concocted for propaganda purposes. As for Huang
Shiren, he was an evil, lascivious landlord character in the opera *Bai-mao nü* (White Feather
Maiden).

SMASHING THE "FOUR OLDS"

The four olds were being smashed, so women could not wear long braids[1]
Because "Chinese girls have amazing dreams / Of uniforms, not trousseaus"!
Our city propaganda team patrolled the streets, spreading the decree
Stern red guards were quick with scissors—lose your braid, not your head
My short-haired revolutionary sister urged our mother to beware
Mother said she wouldn't know how to walk, wouldn't look right without
    them
Sister yielded and only cut her braids three inches shorter
The next day, red guards caught Mother at our door and lopped them off
Auntie Five, who lived next door, hid for three days, not eating, in her room
A neighbor girl brought the red guards; they dragged her out and paraded her
Short-haired women cinching military belts strutted down the street
Wielding scissors, they pounced upon any long-braided ladies
I followed them, picking up the long glossy braids
At the refuse depot I could sell them for two dimes a catty

04:40, November 8, 2012. No.1416 Wembley Road, San Marino, Los Angeles.

---

1. On June 1, 1966, the *People's Daily* editorial "Sweep All Monsters" proposed the slogan
"Get rid of all the old ideas, old culture, old customs, and old habits from the exploiting class-
es that have poisoned our people for thousands of years." Cultivating the "four news" then
meant to establish new ideas, new culture, new customs, and new habits.

SENDING AWAY THE NO-GOODNIKS

In 1967 a crowd formed early one morning outside our city's South Gate
Central was enforcing the people's dictatorial will: all the no-goodniks were
    to be dispersed[1]
Most were youngsters, chattering and tussling, but their parents were
    blank-faced
Knowing what was good for them, they loaded baggage on trucks like
    meek lambs
As enemies of the proletariat, they were being sent to villages to live a hard
    life
They were the underclass of New China, not fit to raise children in the city
He Lili had shared my desk; she was sent to the Gu Mountains of Xihai
I liked her for imagining herself as Qu Tao in the novel *Three-Family Lane*[2]
Her father was deputy to Ma Hongkui;[3] he must have fought the
    Liberation Army
Revolutionaries never forget class hatred or debts of blood
Yi Qing was sent away to a cave house in the mountains
It was on a ridge, without even a door to keep out the wind and sun
All these years later, she does not like to talk, so we call her "Yam-Egg"
I think it's from herding sheep in the mountains, never seeing people
He Lili is hyperactive and talks nonstop, from being kept quiet at home

    05:10, November 8, 2012. 1416 Wembley Road, San Marino, Los Angeles.

---

1. At the beginning of the Cultural Revolution, in many parts of China's territory, families
belonging to the so-called *heiwulei*—"five black categories"—were forced to leave the cities
and move to remote rural areas. The five categories were landlords, the wealthy, counterrevo-
lutionaries, bad elements, and rightists.
2. *Sanjia-xiang* (Three-Family Lane) is a novel by Ouyang Shan.
3. Ma Hongkui, a member of the Northwest warlord group termed "the four Mas," was first
attached to the warlord Feng Yuxiang and later went over to Chiang Kai-shek. He served
as the governor of Ningxia for seventeen years and concentrated full military and political
power in his own hands. Thus he was also known as the "Tyrant of Ningxia."

LI JUN WROTE A PERVERSE SLOGAN

One day "Down with Chairman Mao" was found written in the park toilet
Handwriting was checked citywide, until they nabbed my classmate Li Jun
He actually was the one who had discovered it; he thought it would win
    him merit
The school held an urgent struggle session to make him confess
He was a seventh-grader of good background, so he avoided going to jail
But during the shaming, he wanted to die rather than give up his armband
He knelt and did prostrations; he bit his finger until it bled
After that, he had to show up early; he did cleanup in a white armband
The school assigned an essay topic—"Why Did Li Jun Commit His Crime"
Students and teachers agreed he had done it—it made sense and was
    thought-provoking
Then one day during cleanup, he dropped a ceramic bust of Mao
Our whole class was dumbfounded; he was white as a sheet
He was put on public trial, sentenced to four years in prison
His short frame was bent and trussed; the plaque at his neck touched the floor
Later we heard he'd done time and was released, but he wouldn't leave prison
We heard that his prison work was mostly planting trees and cutting grass

05:37, November 8, 2012. 1416 Wembley Road, San Marino, Los Angeles.

SELF-STUDY UNIVERSITY OF COMMUNISM

It was Wu Shuzhang who founded the "Self-Study University of Communism"
He said, "Cult-Revo is red terror" and "Sending school-kids to farms is just
    labor reform"
They worked in factories during the day, studied Marxism in the evening
They wrote letters asking why the Cultural Revolution had turned bloody
The great Public Security Bureau found their letters; some say there was a
    snitch
That kind of counterrevolutionary incident shook the whole city
Xiong Manli was an electrician; she electrocuted herself before they
    caught her
People said she was smart and pretty, but she liked to read too much
Lu Zhili was a lathe operator; he was sentenced to die by firing squad
Because he tried to shout slogans, they cut his windpipe first
The Wu brothers were paraded under guard in a truck
We ran after them, wanting to watch the firing squad
Big red forks pressed down on their necks, from which plaques were hung
Their execution galvanized the city like a major festival
Being small, I was pushed to the rear; I only heard the gunshots

06:01, November 8, 2012. 1416 Wembley Road, San Marino, Los Angeles.

BLACKSMITH LIU

The fire always burned hot in Blacksmith Liu's forge
Standing in his streetside smithy, he pounded iron, muttering all the while
He was dissatisfied with many things; he sounded like a complainer
Nowadays we would say he was mentally disturbed
Detail-minded neighbors remembered his reactionary remarks
Red guards in disguise observed his every move
Security thought he was a spy for Soviet revisionists, plotting subversion
They thought he was speaking Russian, since no one could understand him
Blacksmith Liu's son was worried; he wanted his dad to close the smithy
Liu went on pounding angrily; "I'll pound that bastard flat," he said
Blacksmith Liu was hauled in, tried in public, then taken out and shot
While being paraded, he kept saying, *those bastards, those bastards*
He wasn't a political prisoner, so they didn't cut his windpipe
A rumor went around—he had been reciting Pushkin poems in Russian
After one round he wouldn't fall, so Public Security riddled him with bullets
Gasping with his eyes half-open, he gave me nightmares for many years

04:22, November 9, 2012. 96 Linda Isle, Newport Beach.

BIG SCOOP LITTLE SCOOP

No one knew her name; they called her Big Scoop Little Scoop
She was an old woman, lean and withered, smoking roll-your-own tobacco
Apparently childless, she combed the streets selling perforated scoops
She yelled, *big scoop, little scoop* while her hands busily twisted the wire mesh
But she also sang that ditty "The sun comes up just a little red"
Everyone in the city had heard her sing it for years
She was wraithlike; even now, no one knows where she came from
Her appearance never changed as she strode through my boyhood years
What a shame she was branded a counterrevolutionary and put to death
She had the gall to insult the red sun for not brightening the whole world
Being illiterate, she had no idea of revolution or proletarian dictatorship
I also think she was too poor to pay the ammo fee before she was shot
Public Security shot her without payment; they fired numerous bullets
But she died from the first bullet to the back of her head
Onlookers lifted her thin clothes to look at her breasts
They were dark and wrinkled, dry and flat like beef jerky

04:43, November 9, 2012. 96 Linda Isle, Newport Beach.

THE BLIND MAN AND HIS WIFE

The blind man lived with his wife across the way
Ours was a little city; we could hear them argue all the time
By day the blind husband pulled a cart while his wife watched the road
They always bickered over what to do about their only son
Their son was a jerk who enjoyed knocking me down
He stole from neighbors and his parents; I think he lived to steal
He was a mean sonofabitch, and even red guards steered clear of him
His parents would act crazy and roll around when their cub got in trouble
He wouldn't rebel or make revolution; to Public Security he was a headache
He cleared out one night before the people's dictatorship could nab him
Someone heard his dad say he'd get bread and butter for fleeing to the Soviets
His dad said that after having sat through many outdoor screenings of
    Lenin in 1918
Some say he fled Ningxia, then got through Inner Mongolia and into
    Mongolia
Some say the Mongolian border guards sent him back with all of his ribs
    broken
Some say he escaped from prison but was buried by snow on the Gobi
Some say the blind man still pulls his cart, but they no longer hear that
    couple talking

05:04, November 9, 2012. 96 Linda Isle, Newport Beach.

HA WENGUI

Our neighbor's oldest son, Ha Wengui, liked to mind other people's business
It bothered him to see red guards shaming eggheads and harrying fat cats
He was strong and a fast walker; I still don't know how he made a living
He wore Huili-brand white tennis shoes—the standard footwear for
    hoodlums
Red guards formed two factions—both were tough and had gotten Mao's
    blessing
They forced every person to choose a side
They lashed the vacillators with steel whips
Those whips of braided wire had bearings at the end; I had one, too
Ha Wengui's whip was thick and long; he wore it at his waist
With a flick of his whip, he could sever a tree as thick as your fist
He was a sworn enemy of red guards, so his death was inevitable
The rival sides plotted together and laid a trap for him
One night they started whipping a capitalist roader
For the sake of justice, Ha Wengui stepped in and warned them back
The whole crowd set upon him and quickly beat him to death
They threw him in a sewer pit, and he froze stiff that night

05:21, November 9, 2012. 96 Linda Isle, Newport Beach.

A SLUT WAS PARADED THROUGH THE STREETS

One other classmate in my homeroom was my mortal enemy
I hit him in the face with a slingshot; he lashed my head with a steel whip
But his sister was pretty, and she often smiled at me
Around her clustered red guards of different factions
She vowed to sleep with all the men on earth, to elevate the position of
     women
Wearing army clothes and short hair, she stayed over at boyfriends' houses
Cult-Revo was a great time for all-out rebellion, so people didn't hold back
Holding a whip, you were master of the world, fighting for Chairman Mao
That pretty Sis had a jackknife—she stuck it in her lovers' legs after sex
She said if they had any balls, they would stick it in her breast
One of them sang like a bird to his dad, who was a rebel leader
The Rebel Faction rounded up pretty Sis and paraded her through the city
They hung worn-out shoes from her neck and smeared her with greasepaint
That was a rousing day in our city; the alleys emptied and the crowds buzzed
Although she bowed her head, I could tell from her face she didn't care
I caught her words: *Mama's boys! If you had any balls, you'd tear my cunt to*
     pieces

05:38, November 9, 2012. 96 Linda Isle, Newport Beach.

TODAY THEY'RE SHOOTING COUNTERREVOLUTIONARIES!

Watching counter-revs get shot was a major form of entertainment in our city
We would run behind the tumbrel truck to get a spot with a view
The execution ground was set up on an untended stretch along Tangxia
    Culvert
The wild jujube trees had a nice smell, showing a golden tinge when ripe
Liberation Army men would plant red flags to mark the spot
The hog-tied culprit would kneel, his neck pressed down by pronged boards
The gun muzzle would touch the back of his head, and we would crowd in
    close
The biggest thrill was when they shot a big group all at once
Once they lined up seventeen people in a long row, male and female
At a wave of the conductor's flag, shots rang out and died away
Security men with pistols turned each body over, making sure
With cotton in tweezers, they checked for breath from the nostrils
Sometimes they would forcefully stomp on a corpse's chest
Or they would give the bodies a second shot, one by one
They walked on blood-spattered dirt, letting us yell: *Shoot her again*
Because we saw that the chest of a female corpse was still heaving

06:02, November 9, 2012. 96 Linda Isle, Newport Beach.

EXECUTION SITE BENEATH THE WALL

Once the killing site was beneath the wall outside our middle school
Too bad there was only one culprit; I couldn't hear his name and crime
The city wall no longer seems high, but it gave us a full-on view
The culprit knelt with his face to the wall, right beneath our feet
People ran at a mad dash, fearing they'd miss the big moment
It was a bit hot and muggy, a bit hard to draw a breath
It made the security men listless to be shooting only one culprit
Going about their business, they scratched a midsized circle in the dirt
The shooter cocked his semi-automatic, touching the muzzle to the
    culprit's head
The two men pressing his head down quickly pulled away their red-
    pronged boards
After the gunshot, the culprit made no move; a security man kicked him over
Lying sideways in the dirt, his mouth gaped and closed
I guess he wanted to say something, or call someone's name
Before I could listen, the security man shot him in the head again
The top of his skull was blown off; a red pennant was stuck in bloody brains
Within an hour, he was stripped and left naked under the sun

06:47, November 9, 2012. 96 Linda Isle, Newport Beach.

A RED GUARD WAS HACKED TO DEATH

I don't fear ghosts, because my generation grew up seeing the dead
Counter-revs shot, landlords beaten, and red guards chopped with cleavers
Once miners and a rebel faction attacked some students guarding the
    West Tower
There was a heated three-day skirmish, but no one had died yet
The students hurled down stones, vowing to defend the Great Leader at
    all costs
The mine workers whetted cleavers and spears
The whole city turned out to cheer and view the battle
Stones and knives did not dull their appetite for revolution
Miners swarmed the wall, trouncing the thuggish students, who were
    only kids
Yielders with raised arms were lashed on the butt and told to scram
A stubborn red guard with a quick slingshot would not give in
Girls looking on cheered him for being a hero, a real he-man
A mine worker snuck up behind him and struck him with a cleaver
He died instantly; his corpse was carried to the military police compound
The military would not mete out justice, claiming they were in a tough spot
The whole city lined up and filed by to see his split head

06:37, November 9, 2012. 96 Linda Isle, Newport Beach.

THE CORPSE IN THE BATHTUB

The corpse in the bathtub belonged to a Rebel Factioneer
The Rebel Faction took his pitchfork-riddled body to the Garrison
They laid him there to prove what cruel reactionaries their enemies were
His body, soaked in formalin, was not decayed or misshapen
It was totally nude and turned sideways to show its punctured ribcage
People filed past the corpse, counting the number of holes
Some people swear they saw its mouth open wide to shout
Others said the corpse could crawl into bed at night and sleep
They said it was a Rebel playing dead, trying to make the army take sides
I went three times, wanting to stick my finger in a puncture wound
I wanted to know how deep a wound it took to make you leave this world
I wanted to turn him over and see if his eyes were closed
To back up my words when I spouted off in front of my buddies
Later the corpse was buried, to the dismay of people in the city
Without a dead man on view, the people didn't know what to do

06:52, November 9, 2012. 96 Linda Isle, Newport Beach.

MA SIYI

Ma Siyi served in the Northwest Underground; later he led the Rebel Faction
He was trapped alone on the roof of the Wuzhong Gauge Factory
The other side hemmed him in for days, but he wouldn't surrender
His buddies hurried night and day from Yinchuan to save him
He could shoot straighter than his enemies, but he couldn't bear to kill
Finally one of them shot him; they dragged his body onto the street
The victors fired guns into the air to celebrate
Someone cut him open and stuffed his belly with bricks
They dragged him through the streets like a dead dog
"Civil attack, martial defense—no one stands against us!"
His grizzled hair was now matted with blood
His underbelly was exposed; some said his penis was small
People on the street spat on him or let their children piss on him . . .
I guess they were treating his corpse as a Cult-Revo battle prize
What happened later to Ma's corpse is unknown
Some say it was eaten by dogs, or torn apart by people

07:13, November 9, 2012. 96 Linda Isle, Newport Beach.

TWO YUAN FOR ONE CORPSE

In August 1967, the Zhangzheng Bridge Rebels ambushed another faction
It was an armed struggle, and they went at it with real knives and guns
The dead were thrown in Xigan Culvert to float with the current
A long club was shoved all the way up one girl's vagina
An old muleteer delightedly fished out bodies and took them to Yinchuan
Two yuan for each body—he got paid when he handed them over
The old man denied that he had stripped one woman's corpse
He said, "Her clothes were split from two days of swelling"
In the city people waited by the road, watching for bodies
Some laughed and some cried; some kept a running total
They needed the old man's mule wagon to help move the bodies
As money changed hands, plans of vengeance were hatched
I confess that I inspected each corpse carefully
I kept track of male or female, and wounds to head or chest
I noticed the old man on his wagon, grinning to himself
Thinking what an easy business this was, two yuan for one corpse

07:30, November 9, 2012. 96 Linda Isle, Newport Beach.

THE BATTLE AT ZHANGZHENG BRIDGE[1]

The ambushers did not make a sound until the first shot
I heard they were demobilized guerillas, well-trained with nerves of steel
They shot to wipe out the other faction, for the Great Leader's sake
They made sure each bullet hit home, to serve the cause of revolution
The Rebel Faction charged, making themselves targets like Huang Jiguang[2]
They yelled, *Long live Chairman Mao, we will never retreat!*
Knife-waving girls let out shrill cries just before they fell
They wailed and screamed, *Don't let the bastards get away!*
That was August 30, 1967, when the sorghum was just turning red
That was under an autumn sky, so gunshots rang out clearly
No one yielded on the Cult-Revo battlefield, for this was a great revolution
Mao's fighters stayed loyal and saw this revolution through to the end
Before they shoved something up her vagina, one girl cried, *No man has
    touched me*
She begged, *I want to die fast . . . let me be clean!*
People in a nearby field heard her; others say they didn't
She was thrown in the culvert to float back toward the city

07:45, November 9, 2012. 96 Linda Isle, Newport Beach.

---

1. On August 30, 1967, the "Headquarters" faction and the "Grand Coalition Preparatory
Office" faction in Yinchuan, Ningxia, engaged in an armed conflict that became known as
"the Battle at Zhangzheng Bridge."
2. Huang Jiguang (1931–1952) was a Chinese war hero who was killed in action during the
Korean Conflict.

CANNON FIRE AT QINGTONG GORGE

Demented miners wanted to breach the dam and drown the city's rebels
They built a stockade and hauled explosives up to the dam
Being loyal to Chairman Mao, they intended to control Cult-Revo
They wanted to make sure Mao could hear their voices in Beijing
Amid citywide terror, the 62nd Brigade hauled out large cannons
The miners said, *We workers are the vanguard of Cult-Revo; who dares
       oppose us?*
They chased away army messengers after smearing their faces black
They fired off rounds before the cannons to show defiance
They were going to light the fuse when a shell blew them to heaven
They howled and scrambled away, leaving a heap of bodies
Artillery rounds hit their mark with deadly efficiency
The miners fell heavily on top of each other, dead in an instant
They died before they had time to shout, *Long live Chairman Mao*
Some were blown to bits while still holding liquor glasses
Soldiers charged through the rising smoke—*Hand over your arms!*
Red flags waved; gunfire shook the sky; the Yellow River surged

08:01, November 9, 2012. 96 Linda Isle, Newport Beach.

THE ARMORY RAID

When the Garrison Armory was raided, most of the soldiers had withdrawn
The other rebel faction claimed the army was in cahoots with the raiders
Lots of people had guns and used them, going around with a cocky attitude
They shot at the sky, at people, at animals—it was a hail of bullets
People would sneak into the armory at night and haul out ammo
They fired rounds wastefully, to sell the bullet casings for scrap
My hobby was collecting bullets left behind by target shooters
Bullets could be melted down for lead and sold at a good price
I didn't blink at gunfire, and I could identify guns by type
Thanks to Cult-Revo, a teenager grew up under the shadow of gun barrels
Once a shooter's gun misfired and hit my classmate in the leg
He sat down crying—*Why didn't you watch out for me?*
They were grappling with the gun and it went off again
This time it hit the shooter's foot—his eyes were staring wide
After that, I handled guns carefully and watched where I pointed them
Of course, I would never let anyone point a gun at my eye

08:23, November 9, 2012. 96 Linda Isle, Newport Beach.

CHEN XUERU

Chen Xueru headed one rebel faction; he had a commanding presence
A former truck driver, he had risen to the top in a single bound
With a gun on his hip, he commanded thousands of troops
His armed patrols took charge of public order in the city
If his underlings tangled with the army, he'd take a soldier prisoner
He had a machine gun nest on his roof, ready for battle
One day he got cornered in a house, trading shots with the other side
He shot the skin of his belly and played dead; he was taken to the hospital
This has to be a prime example of life snatched from the jaws of death
History and revolution need heroes, just as they need scoundrels
A Revolutionary Committee formed, ranking him second, a seeming success
But some say restless ghosts were at work, to bring him within reach of
    revenge
Of course I believe it, because later all the rebels were called out for their
    crimes
I had seen Chen Xueru's group march through the streets with guns blazing
Later I saw him bound with thick ropes, paraded in front of crowds

08:41, November 9, 2012. 96 Linda Isle, Newport Beach.

LIU QINGSHAN

This is also a real person's name—he was the ringleader of a rebel faction
He led armed struggles and killed plenty of people
Even the army steered clear of him; he had the other side running scared
He had a devil-may-care attitude, always packing two Mauser pistols
He liked women and didn't care what rumors were spread about him
His wife made terrible scenes, but for some reason he didn't have her shot
Mothers liked him because children would stop fretting and wait to see him
Women liked him because his mistresses could have their way in the city
Once he was surrounded by a huge force; he stood on a roof returning fire
With perfect aim, he killed the other side's leader and won the day
Later he too was rounded up and put in prison; I think he died there of illness
Some people say he had syphilis from too much womanizing
After he was locked up, no one dared mention his name
He even admitted that once he got out, he would still feel driven to kill
But some people said he was an upright fellow—a firm, unselfish rebel
He was the only one who saw the revolution through to the end

08:55, November 9, 2012. 96 Linda Isle, Newport Beach.

THE OUTCOME OF THE KILLINGS

Later came the era of purges, because someone had to answer for homicide
There were written or oral records about who beat whom to death
A student who beat his classmate to death was sentenced and shot right away
There was no mortal hatred between them, just loyalty to Chairman Mao
That was a time that enraged people and set them against each other
The killer locked my classmate in a dark room to be punished
He made the boy get down on all fours and beat him with a club
He would not stop until the boy renounced his wrong views
The boy would only cry, *Long live Chairman Mao, down with conservatives*
He also said, *Mao's fighters don't surrender*, then coughed up blood and fainted
He was taken to the hospital, but his kidneys had ruptured
He couldn't urinate, so his family rushed him to a Beijing-bound train
He died on the train, which was slow and running behind schedule
He was only twenty, still wearing his red armband and Mao badge
The twenty-one-year-old killer did not escape death, either
His kin refused his body, so it was given to an anatomy class

09:08, November 9, 2012. 96 Linda Isle, Newport Beach.

THE ARMY REPRESENTATIVE

Turn the tables by stepping up production! Make revolution by resuming
    classes!
The army rep came to our school and led the criticism of Lin Biao and
    Confucius
Qiu Zhongfen was an officer's wife, so she lorded it over everyone
We were assigned to squads and platoons, under army-style command
Because of Qiu's small stature, teachers constantly had to bow before her
She had the power to send any teacher off to a work farm
She judged whether students were good or bad based on their family
    backgrounds
She barely deigned to glance in my direction
Most of her favorites were accepted by the army
Luckily she rejected me, or I wouldn't be on the Forbes list now
In class we critiqued enemies of Marxism-Leninism and Mao Zedong
    Thought
We were told that socialist hay was better than capitalist wheat sprouts
Anything the enemy was for, we were supposed to be against
My middle-school years were spent under the guidance of this army rep
As I did then, I still refer to Qiu Zhongfen as "Fileface Qiu"
When I think of her, I have only curses, for her and for that era

09:37, November 9, 2012. 96 Linda Isle, Newport Beach.

THE WORKERS' PROPAGANDA TEAM

"The workers will take full charge" was the slogan of that period
So a workers' propaganda team took over everything at our school
The team leader was a classic sex fiend, with a constant bulge in his pants
Thinking back now, I know he was just a worker, not much older than twenty
Under false pretenses he would have heart-to-heart talks with female students
That awkward sign of his arousal made the male students giggle
He never gave me a kind look, because I liked to make trouble
He said I should own up to being a counterrevolutionary's son
A few times I thought he wanted to hit me, but he held back
Because I glowered at him, ready for an all-out fight
I disdained him for not knowing about Tolstoy or Pushkin
He was irritated by my sharp-tongued eloquence
At one point he was going to expel me, but he changed his mind
Because I knew he had handed a love letter to a girl student
I dared not hate one of the working class, but I hated that rotten era
Someone always wanted to occupy the open ground of our youth

09:48, November 9, 2012. 96 Linda Isle, Newport Beach.

I WAS AN UNDERGROUND ARMS MAKER

Later I learned to make a zip gun and went on hunting excursions
But I never hit so much as a small sparrow with it
Being rebellious and having no books to read, I stirred up trouble
I used my gun to shatter windows at our school
While testing my gun, I shot someone's bike tire by accident
The police station sent men to my classroom to haul me in
Public Security made sure I hadn't robbed or killed, then sent me back
The authority figures at my school all wanted to expel me
They held meetings for days to let the teachers and students critique me
That was Cult-Revo, so I had no sense of shame or dignity
But they ultimately decided to keep me in school for observation
I think they were worried I'd do something unpleasant or desperate
But I refused to wear a white armband and do cleanup in contrition
Fileface Qiu said, "I'll make sure this stays in your file forever"
When I went to college, I hand-delivered my file, but I broke it open first
I found her stamped sheet of paper and used it for toilet paper

10:00, November 9, 2012. 96 Linda Isle, Newport Beach.

HOUSEHOLD REGISTRY CHECK

Public Security had power; they could enter your home at will to check papers
Often they would barge in at night and ask to see your registry booklet
I was the troublemaking son of a traitor, so they had me in their sights
One security man would drag me from my bed and ask what I'd been up to
I couldn't stand it, so one day I grabbed the man's son and slapped him
Then I was questioned every night; the neighbors were told I was a crime
    suspect
By day I glared at him on the street and uttered obscenities
He feared I would bash his son's head in, so he gave me a chilling smile
At my school he spread word that I was a hoodlum
I was a scandalous figure, and my female classmates kept their distance
He said I was a stalker, a peeping tom, and a petty thief
He said a porno pin-up of the folk heroine Ashima hung on my wall
I had been a red guard; I was fearless and wild to the bone
For instance, I'd yell, *Who's afraid of you? All I have is this rotten life!*
I waited a long time: one night he dutifully came to check our papers
As he pushed the door open, a basin of shit fell onto his head

10:13, November 9, 2012. 96 Linda Isle, Newport Beach.

THE BOOK THIEF

During Cult-Revo, anything could be a poisonous weed of feudalism,
    bourgeois thinking, or revisionism
Everyone was criticizing absolute music and Shakespeare
Yet I turned into a book thief who pried open a library door
Then I became famous in our city as a source of books
I always had literary works to offer in private trades
I had a world of my own, although I came by it through stealing
I would weep all night for the Gadfly, or feel anxious for the Count of
    Monte Cristo
I went wild over Mark Twain and could recite from *A Hunter's Diary*
Late at night, I would sit and muse about becoming a poet
After barbarous acts, I would dream of refinement
Thanks to the treasury of books that I found in that era
They made me want to become a person with dignity
After writing a poem, I might punch a classmate in the nose
After reading *Dream of Red Mansions*, I might pour ink down a girl's blouse
Now I think the good side of book thievery outweighed the bad side
It helped me learn how to save myself in that troubled era

10:25, November 9, 2012. 96 Linda Isle, Newport Beach.

A SECRET LISTENER TO ENEMY BROADCASTS

The one who actually listened to enemy broadcasts was my mother
She would get up at night and put on the earphones of her crystal radio
I could hear continuous code numbers from a Taiwan station
Or voices from the powerful broadcasts of Soviet revisionists
I don't know what Mother listened to or what she was thinking
By day she hauled dirt to sell, keeping to herself in our little city
Back then the enemy stations seemed clearer than our revolutionary stations
After listening, Mother gave no sign of what she felt
But I had nightmares that security men would burst in and catch her
I feared the neighbors would report her; she would be paraded through
    the streets
One day a neighbor really did turn in another neighbor
Security men ransacked their house; their workplace kicked them out
Their daughter was my classmate; she had to withdraw from school
The family was sent to a mountain district, never to be heard from again
Later Mother still got up at night, but simply leaned against the wall
After that, I never saw her get out her crystal radio set

10:41, November 9, 2012. 96 Linda Isle, Newport Beach.

CRITIQUING ABSOLUTE MUSIC

Xin Fei and I once planned to beat up Chen Jian, the violinist for an opera troupe

His wife, Yu Fang, had friction both on- and offstage with my classmate Qu Ailing

But Chen Jian raised his violin and played a piece that brought tears to my eyes

He said, "Don't you know this? It's 'Dying Swan' by Saint-Saens"

He said, "You mustn't tell people I've been playing absolute music

Recently Beijing called for it to be critiqued as bourgeois culture"

We all had to sing model opera, recite Mao quotes, dance the drill-team dance

Violinists had to play "Beijing News Reaches a Border Town" or "Horse Race"

Once I knew about Beethoven, I couldn't get enough of *Eroica*

That's why I broke open a library window, so I could find the record

We would close the room up tight and sit on a bed listening to absolute music

Beauty and amazement are hard to talk about, but we said, "not bad" or "interesting"

Later Chen dropped out of sight—maybe he was busy struggling or critiquing

After I got rich, I had two-meter speakers installed at home, for classical music only

When I fly, I still get teary-eyed listening to "Dying Swan"

Thanks to Cult-Revo for critiques that helped me discover what was precious!

10:11, November 17, 2012. 96 Linda Isle, Newport Beach.

RED DETACHMENT OF WOMEN

Red Detachment of Women was a model opera produced by Jiang Qing
She was Mao Zedong's old lady, so she wanted to edify the whole nation
Red Detachment of Women was performed by ballet dancers, so it appealed
    to male viewers
The jealous head of a rebel faction once pulled out a gun and shot "Wu
    Qingxia" in the leg
The women in the detachment all had nice figures, which made us all wish
    for revolution
Just think—the revolution made Chinese women even bolder than men
Thus the dream lover of every Chinese male was Wu Qingxia
Thus the perfect idol of every Chinese female was Yang Zirong
We praised the revolution for its big, strong men, for its swashbuckling
    women
I really liked *Red Detachment* for all those attractive faces
The whole country watched those model operas for years and never tired
    of them
That was because we grasped the idea of revolution, and these were its
    exemplars
After Jiang Qing's suicide, I continued to hum the aria from "Dragon River"
I think my life originated from revolutionary genes
Even now I sing "Beams of light shine everywhere from Gold Hill in Beijing"
Once you've been a red guard, I think your fists stay clenched for a lifetime

11:02, November 9, 2012. 96 Linda Isle, Newport Beach.

THE SPOOKY CATHOLIC CHURCH

We all knew that dead infants were hidden in the basement of the Catholic
    church
Citizens swarmed behind the red guards who charged in to search the place
The nuns were not pretty, but they were calm from praying to Jesus
The bleeding man on the cross looked down in grief at us all
Red guards demolished pews for firewood; smoke rose from burning Bibles
Some said they heard babies crying, sending a shiver up our spines
The bishop explained that the wind was howling; in fact he was sobbing inside
Though they may smash, kill, and burn, the Lord loves all the people
There was not much to see, so I grabbed a Bible to use as toilet paper
But that night I read stories of Cain losing his way, of desert snakes
Even now I am not a believer, but I feel a twinge of guilt
Stealing that Bible and destroying church property may keep me out of
    heaven
Once I got rich, I went back home to do something for that church
I wouldn't say to save my soul, but wanting the Lord to think kindly of me
Now office buildings tower along the streets, with no sign of that Catholic
    church
Someone said, "Developers like you got rich from tearing down old buildings"
I think maybe the Lord's feelings had been hurt, and he felt like moving
    anyway

17:56, November 19, 2012. Asakusa Hall of Valley Fishpond, Beijing Kunlun Hotel.

AN EMBROIDERED SLIPPER

My city is in the West, so winters are harsh and cheerless
Even so, I stood in a doorway to hear about the embroidered slipper
It was an era of one against all, with few warm sentiments
But at least we could hear stories to help us ignore those tough times
Good old Yu Nian, my classmate in tenth grade, was a natural storyteller
I would lie in bed at night reliving a plot as chills went up my spine
After he told about a dead man on a bus, I dared not ride buses anymore
When he told the story of the embroidered slipper, we would huddle
    around him
When he told about Carmen, I wept and had waking dreams about her
I was no longer a red guard at night but a dreamy youth
I never figured out what happened to the embroidered slipper
As I grew up, it became my personal memorial of an era
Later I learned that Carmen was a gypsy woman
She was a pretty, wild sexpot who liked the richest upper-crust men
Model operas by day and stories of slippers by night—we lived on both edges
That was an era; those were our days; that was our kind of remembrance

13:15, November 9, 2012. 96 Linda Isle, Newport Beach.

CHICKEN BLOOD INJECTIONS

Liu Xiaobao's dad got a shot of chicken blood, and he found it energizing
He said it was due to the rooster's strength, because it had never mated
The neighbors pooled their money and went to purchase roosters in the
    countryside
The city was full of men strutting briskly to work
A line of men with roosters formed at the hospital door
Doctors busily stuck needles into chickens, drawing blood for injections
I don't know if anyone died later, but a fad was underway
In a materialistic time, what else did people have to do?
People said the shots made their bodies lighter, gave their steps more bounce
It made eyes bright, minds clear, faces youthful, and hair like crane feathers
Some said it would bring you a plump baby who wouldn't suffer as you had
Some said it kept you from getting hit by bullets in armed struggles
Liu Xiaobao's brother wouldn't get those shots, lest he start crowing or
    pecking
All over the city, people discussed how he had fallen behind the times
They said, "Going to college did him no good—it only made him stupid"

13:47, November 9, 2012. 96 Linda Isle, Newport Beach.

RED KOMBUCHA

Kombucha is a fungus that thrives on tea; the whole city acquired a taste
    for it
It would not be fitting for revolutionary people to be divided in their
    preferences
Revolutionary Committeemen drank it onstage while extolling the
    dictatorship of proles
The revolutionary masses in the audience sipped from mugs while mulling
    big ideas
Lots of girls knitted thermal cup holders out of synthetic yarn
It was a nice touch to prevent scalding, so you could drink kombucha all day
It was a perfect life-prolonging energizer, as everyone believed
How wonderful is the uniformity of people's habits in a revolutionary era!
Niu Keli's father boasted about a special fungus strain he had bred
In fact he had simply put brick tea out in the sun to spoil
Some people got diarrhea—he claimed that would purge their toxins
Before long, people were lining up at his door to buy his prized tea fungus
He was given promotions and ended up with a seat on the Revolutionary
    Committee
But he contracted dysentery and was rushed to the hospital for IV treatment
The ward was overcrowded with people on antibiotics

19:55, November 9, 2012. 96 Linda Isle, Newport Beach.

REPORTING OFFENSES

When Chairman Mao died, the masses grieved across the nation, as did I
But Teacher Li's daughter drew the curtains and went on practicing violin
She was playing the sad, haunting music of Paganini
Teacher Ma indignantly reported this reactionary act to Revo-Comm
Public Security arrested the girl, but they didn't know how to sentence her
Because Teacher Li's wife said it was a sign of grief for the Leader
But we all knew that Teacher Li's family had been ruined by Cult-Revo
They had never shouted, *Long, long live Chairman Mao!*
Teacher Li even said that old-time emperors had also promoted the cult of
    personality
In a new society, we should not go in for such feudal superstition
So the neighbors all willingly conducted surveillance on him
They reported every move by Teacher Li to the organization
Teacher Li also reported his neighbors for singing pornographic folk songs
People were on their guard against each other; everyone was hell for
    everyone else
I also reported my classmate Qu Ailing for bourgeois thinking
Which offenses get reported is a sign of how safe the lives of citizens are

20:14, November 9, 2012. 96 Linda Isle, Newport Beach.

XIN FEI'S BOWLING BALL

Xin Fei's snowy hair shows the ravages of time
He has a heavy bowling ball that he rolls with deadly aim
We used to regret being too small to join the city's armed struggles
We envied those rebel brothers and sisters who went at it with real weapons
We ran behind the tumbrel truck to get good spots at the execution ground
We kept far enough back that the brains wouldn't splatter on us
He always had a copy of *Reference News*, so I was glad to be his sidekick
He explained Hegel to me, and he would sing "My Sunshine" facing the wall
For the struggle with Soviet revisionists, he suggested tractors with flame
    throwers
He appropriated the gun I made, but together we dug an air-raid shelter
We went to college on the Worker-Peasant-Soldier Plan, he to Shanghai, I
    to Beijing
We were called the lost generation, and people averted their eyes from us
After college he went back to Ningxia and ran a paper called *Broadcast News*
He designed and wrote it and did the legwork to sell ads
Now the new leaders don't like him, because he won't admit he's getting old
I say, "In this post–Cult-Revo Era, we should step back and observe"
He says, *No!* . . . He says it still gives him a thrill to think about that era

       November 12, 2012. 1416 Wembley Road, San Marino, Los Angeles.

CARMEN AS TOLD BY OLD YU NIAN

When I was ten years old, Old Yu Nian told us stories from *Carmen* every day
In those days we were entranced by that fetching gypsy femme
As if he were Carmen's little brother, he brought her to life before our eyes
I don't recall that he ever mentioned her death; he just let the story continue
We were in different street gangs during Cult-Revo, but never got in a fight
Because of Carmen, we viewed him in a different light and called him brother
His brother was badly beaten during armed struggle—he died on a train to
    Beijing
Later the killer was sentenced to death, so the blood debt was paid
I always feel sad about our lot in life, being cannon fodder for an era
We were innocent, and what we went through was a crying shame
Fortunately he wasn't sent to a work brigade, which might have limited his
    achievements
He became increasingly silent, I think because of the pressures of life
Later he worked for me in Beijing, but he put up an unlicensed building
At least it was used to raise chickens, so a few birds were free of toxic additives
But I still remember his Carmen stories, and that he helped bury my mother
Now he's holding on in his native place, gradually getting old
I'd like to bring him to Beijing, give him a chance to work for me again

06:32, November 12, 2012. 1416 Wembley Road, San Marino, Los Angeles.

LI BING HAS DROPPED OUT OF SIGHT

I gave Li Bing the nickname Donkey because of his rampant sex drive
I knew about his rich amorous history, and it made me terribly envious
As a child he did not get in fights but was always ready for mischief
As a little red guard he excelled at debate, throwing in expressive gestures
Being jealous, I thought him shameless for scoring with all kinds of girls
Meanwhile, his first girlfriend's child was said to look just like him
Sent to a production team, he put in solid hours, but had time for affairs
He stepped into his father's place, but mainly worked at chasing women
He was good at relating juicy details about his liaisons
I was good at acting shocked, urging him to straighten up
He didn't go to college, so he led his decadent life in Yinchuan
On a visit home we had some drinks, and he hugged me like a maudlin
    donkey
Later his wife taught piano; he was a family man in charge of collecting fees
At our next get-together, he was nervous about getting home late
Evidently his wife thought I was a bad influence on him
I think he must have told her stories about my promiscuous ways
But there's no way to prove this, for Li Bing has dropped out of sight

06:51, November 12, 2012. 1416 Wembley Road, San Marino, Los Angeles.

ZHANG LIN, WHO BECAME TOP LEADER

I am a little red guard who got rich, and Zhang Lin is the leader of our
province
We assembled to receive supreme directives, and we ran a school newsletter
I don't recall him fighting, but he recalls my prank that unseated a cyclist
We lived as we did, and it's hard to say who was bad or good
Zhang Lin didn't join the armed struggles; he was always absorbed in
reading books
Perhaps he understood Marxism-Leninism from a different angle than we did
Zhang Lin didn't write big-character posters, because he disdained them
Now I think it was because, like me, he wasn't much good at calligraphy
After being sent down, he led his commune's opera troupe—a bevy of
pretty girls
On some pretext or other, I would go visit him so I could watch the rehearsals
At Yinchuan Hotel we mounted an exhibit: "Socialism Is Advancing and
Winning"
When he explained Marx's *Contra-Dühring*, my ignorance made me feel
irritated
Chuckling, he'd point at me and say, "You'll soak up plenty if you read more"
Back then I knew he had the look of a leader, and indeed he has climbed high
He invites me to talk about old times over glasses of his own vintage wine
The label on the bottle shows him smiling, and I say he hasn't changed
Those days have passed, and we're lucky the times didn't weed us out

05:30, November 16, 2012. Changhe-wan in Beijing.

WEI XING'S SISTER

Wei Xing and I were buddies; we stuck together like body and shadow
When we stole chickens, he'd crawl into the coop while I kept lookout
Of course, in his compound he would decide when to pull off the heist
As little red guards we went around with slingshots, wearing army belts
Once we put a gash in a ruffian's head
His uncle came close to burying me alive
One time Fileface Qiu drove a wedge between us
Saying I had ratted on Wei Xing for stealing a volleyball
Wei Xing's sister had a low opinion of me; she wouldn't look at me
Yet she let me fill up many times on meals from her kitchen
After being sent down, we lost touch and forgot each other's faces
He stayed on and became leader of our home city's waterworks
When we met again, I could see he drank and smoked heavily
His face and teeth were discolored, but he was still his earnest self
I realized his heart was never as full of guile as mine
Perhaps his sister's view of me was not wrong
In that era we were not ourselves; I was not myself

07:07, November 12, 2012. 1416 Wembley Road, San Marino, Los Angeles.

HE LILI'S OLDER BROTHER

He Lili is a deep ache in my heart, and my dear childhood playmate
Of course I can say this now that she's a grandma, living on her own
When we "made revolution by resuming classes," we shared a desk
I carved the number "38" between us,[1] but let her peek at my test answers
When the class critiqued me, she stepped forward and said I'd been wronged
The boy students were dumbstruck when she showed up early that morning
I felt she was my own Qu Tao,[2] but didn't know that was called infatuation
I was sent down to Tonggui, she to Wuzhong, where I couldn't see her
I missed her and worked up the nerve to write tender letters, but got no
    answer
Later she explained—her big brother did not want us to be in contact
The union of a KMT child with a counter-rev's child would have been
    disastrous
Our fate was changed by Cult-Revo, but we could not change Cult-Revo
I guess that would count as a tragic fate, or a curse there was no escaping
He Lili once headed the Salt Industries Bureau, but she's retired now
She speaks of my poem on a candy wrapper, a handful of mountain jujubes
Her son works for me so he can "toughen up" and maybe make a better life
    for himself
I don't say much, wanting to let her talk more about those days

07:45, November 12, 2012. 1416 Wembley Road, San Marino, Los Angeles.

---

1. As a result of the Korean War, a dividing line was drawn between North Korea and South Korea at the 38th parallel.
2. Qu Tao is a female character in the novel *Sanjia-xiang* by Ouyang Shan.

"NATIONALLY CERTIFIED STAGE MANAGER" QU AILING

Ailing is a true stalwart who created the stage show at our Hong Village
    heritage site
You see, she joined an opera troupe in seventh grade . . . became a class one
    stage manager
She and He Lili were sworn sisters; I suspect the same boy chased them in
    succession
Fate did not bring me together with these beauties, which left me broken-
    hearted for years
Years ago I watched her dance onstage, then lay awake and dreamed for hours
Later she liked my close friend, whose name I still cannot mention
During Cult-Revo I was sent down; she danced in *Red Detachment of Women*
They grew up to be stunners—they became the two scenic wonders of our
    city
She surely had her share of love stories, but won't admit them to me
Later she agreed to produce stage shows for my company
At meetings I would chortle, "Finally I can let out some frustration
I can chide such a personage as He Lili for being long-winded, and I can call
    even Qu Ailing a dimwit"
But bitter times are unforgettable just because of their bitterness
The craziest times are memorable because of their craziness
I hate those days, but I can rejoice now that we're doing all right
I like to watch Ailing with mike in hand, teaching actors how to strike poses
When we fly somewhere together, I like to gripe at her for not liking me
    back then

      08:10, November 12, 2012. 1416 Wembley Road, San Marino, Los Angeles.

ZHANG BINGHE'S SMILE

Though he has worn that smile since boyhood, he used to be quite a fighter
He was sent to a different commune; when I'd visit, he liked to play with my
  gun
I served as brigade bookkeeper; not being a quick talker, he worked in the
  fields
But he did not shoot and kill dogs, as I did, or throw thirteen grenades into
  a cesspool
I had stronger Cult-Revo genes and was more struggle-minded than he was
We used to steal red guard armbands and tear down other people's posters
We also strung up hobbling rope to make cyclists tumble in narrow alleys
In fights he was out front, using deadly fists, while I yelled and jumped around
Now he's in business; he runs an accounting firm that handles audits
Over drinks we marvel at the era we survived, which he recalls more clearly
  than I
When I flash my grin on TV or create a stir on the Web, he knows about it
He helped rebuild my mother's grave and set up a kindergarten I sponsored
Lately we've decided to build a winery on Helan Mountain, just for fun
Since we've come this far, we should have a spot for drinking and talking
We start with red guard times, all the meanness and kindness, recalling who
  survived
We say, "Luckily we did well and don't have to scrimp like some of our
  classmates"
With a smile Zhang says, "We should invite them all for three days of
  drinking"

23:51, November 14, 2012. Seat 1A on Flight CA984 from Los Angeles to Beijing.

CULT-REVO AS LIU SHENGXIN LIVED IT

After college he lived across from me; when Cult-Revo came, he was given
    a rural post
I don't think he ever took part in armed strife; he had time to putter around
    in our courtyard
When people went in for "civil assault," he never read the posters, thinking
    the style muddled
When there were armed struggles, he shut the gate against stray bullets and
    wounded fighters
I still don't understand why he wasn't dragged off and forced to take a side
He rarely mentioned Chairman Mao, just wanted me to find novels he
    could read
He stayed beyond reach of knives, bullets, and purges
He didn't suffer reprisals from those who regained power—he was no one's
    concern
Later he said he had foreseen that Cult-Revo would bring disaster upon all
    the people
The zealous would have bad luck, and the makers of revolution would be
    squashed
Yet the Zhenbao Island incident[1] triggered his zeal, and we dug a shelter in
    the yard
He insisted on making it deep, so all the residents could hide during air raids
I won't forget his surprise at reading my poem "Mayakovsky's Ladder"
He said, "You'll go far. Keep at it, and don't mess around outside"
Now he's old and stays detached from worldly things, so it's hard to say
    what he does
We went grave-sweeping on Helan Mountain; he made prostrations to my
    mother
He said, "I'm here to visit, Auntie. Don't worry, your son is going places"

00:31, November 14, 2012. Seat 1A on Flight CA984 from Los Angeles to Beijing.

---

1. Zhenbao Island (Russian Остров Даманский) is located along the central navigation
channel of the Heilongjiang River, also called the Amur River. In 1969 Chinese and Soviet
military forces clashed due to a disagreement regarding territorial jurisdiction over the is-
land, and Chinese forces established control. This incident marked a low point in deteriorat-
ing Chinese-Soviet relations, which had been friendly in the 1950s and early 1960s.

LIU XIAOBAO'S MARRIAGE PHOTO

Liu Xiaobao was Liu Shengxin's brother—we were pals and did some pilfering
We devoured all the pigeons around the West Gate, because they didn't sell
    for much
During parades, we would use small slingshots to shoot girls in the butt
People would yell, *Hooray for the Great Proletarian Cultural Revolution!*
I used to get beaten at home, and he taught me how to stay out of reach
When my mother or sister reached for the duster, I'd scramble onto the roof
His quiet, serious dad would order him to stand still for a talk, saying
"In these years of mass violence, poor folks shouldn't have illusions"
But we felt rebellion was right, plus it ended our homework and self-criticisms
And we could have gang fights, harry the principal, strap bayonets to our
    waists
Side by side we fought our last gang fight, then we were sent down to
    endure labor
I later heard he was recruited to wear a railroad worker's uniform
In 1978 he visited me at Peking U; we took a souvenir photo at No-Name
    Lake
Next day he asked me to join him; he was going to see Tiananmen and pose
    for a marriage photo with his wife
He said, "Finally I'm here at Tiananmen," but he appeared unmoved
He looked at Mao Zedong's portrait in silence, without his eyes watering
He said, "Let's go; we have to catch the train home and go to work tomorrow"

00:52, November 14, 2012. Seat 1A on Flight CA984 from Los Angeles to Beijing.

LIU XIAOPING'S MISSING TEETH

Lose your front teeth and you'll be ridiculed, like my classmate Liu Xiaoping
Although branded a fat cat, he still talked tough, so his grandpa must have
    had clout
On our way to school, we'd pass his house in the park and yell, *Gap-Toothed
    Liu!*
They'd been knocked out in a cycling mishap, and dental restoration was
    rare then
For us rebellion meant cursing and fighting and spitting in the principal's face
Quick-tongued Liu liked to debate with rebel red guards on the street all
    night
Once he scraped the surface off a Mao badge while shimmying down a tree
He begged me to keep his secret and promised to find a new one by the
    next day
He got it by snatching it from the chest of a girl red guard
People yelled, *Catch that thief,* but he'd planned his escape through the woods
He was odd and standoffish toward people, always talking about his grandpa
After his grandpa took the second spot in Revo-Comm, he was more
    high-handed
Later I practiced a quick jab and landed a blow on his chin
I emerged the victor in our many-year rivalry, and many people cheered me
Later he married our school beauty Chen Xiaoqin, displeasing his classmates
They grumble that due to strict rules at home, she can never come to a
    reunion
Now he is a section head, lording it over folks and deploring their tight-
    fistedness

00:57, November 14, 2012. Seat 1A on Flight CA984 from Los Angeles to Beijing.

BLACK-BEARDED NING HAN

When I talk about this person I feel disgust, because of his bushy black beard
A bigger reason is that he once wore my hat on his foot to amuse our class
I couldn't beat him in a fight, because he was always surrounded by a gang
  of cadres' sons
But I lived in a slum and wore patched clothes, and I had snot on my sleeve
They occupied themselves in Cult-Revo by picking fights with other tough
  punks
They attacked the fathers of rival gang members, plotting to ransack each
  other's houses
In parades we marched on different sides, each with our own banner
We chanted revolutionary slogans more resoundingly than anyone
When Revo-Comm was formed, their fathers were brought into the
  revolution's camp
Avoiding farm work, Ning was hired by Public Security, helped by his
  deputy-chief father
In the Hainan Boom he headed the Anti-Mob Office, but ended up joining
  the mob himself
He kept stolen goods and put people under house arrest on trumped-up
  charges
Later he came home and remarried; he was a house husband who lived off
  his wife
He crashed all his classmates' banquets, boasting as he ate and drank his fill
He even phoned my company, saying he was my classmate and wanted to
  see me
He must have been desperate—thought he would try his luck at bumming
  money
To hell with that hoodlum who only prolongs the vile legacy of Cult-Revo

01:14, November 14, 2012. Seat 1A on Flight CA984 from Los Angeles to Beijing.

SONG QIANG THE POLICEMAN

I truly miss Song Qiang, who was my good buddy in junior middle school
He lived in a dorm of the MP Garrison Hospital, and his parents were friendly
His father didn't yell, "He's some kind of ruffian; we don't want him in the
    house"
Of course, I was never asked to join them for dinner
Song Qiang never demonstrated in the streets or put up posters
He never went with me to public trials and executions
But he took me to the specimen room and showed me a human skeleton
He furtively watched to see if I would tremble in fear
An army doctor had dissected a dead counter-rev, to practice flaying skin
Mounted on the wall, it looked huge—nailed there as if it might run away
The doctor put the body parts in a basin and buried them near a culvert
Song Qiang knew the place and secretly took me there more than once
I didn't notice that the grass there grew any differently than the grass nearby
Later the executed man was absolved, and his family dug up that spot in vain
I dared not mention the skin to anyone, not wanting to cause trouble
After working on a farm, Song became a policeman who is said to have a
    thing for handcuffs
He hasn't come to any gatherings or met with me, perhaps for fear I'd ask
    about that skin

01:41, November 14, 2012. Seat 1A on Flight CA984 from Los Angeles to Beijing.

ZHANG YAN'S BALD HEAD

As a child, Zhang Yan had big eyes and red lips, so women found him adorable

Due to a lack of self-esteem, I said he was a sissy who wouldn't amount to much

During Cult-Revo, he didn't get into mischief and he didn't perform revolutionary deeds

He was peaceful and well-behaved, always sitting at his courtyard gate

He watched street demonstrations; he watched armed struggles and funeral processions

People who saw him would say, "Look at that cute little thing"

We didn't move in the same circles, but now and then we traded books

He never said bad things about me, so I didn't spread rumors about him

I haven't heard whether he joined a rural production team—that was a hard life, for sure

I still don't get this statement—*That is a broad expanse where much can be achieved*

Luck was with him, and he rose to be head of the TV station, an important figure

I saw him—plump and bald—acting aloof toward those who did his bidding

What a blow for me: as a poet I should say, *Scoundrel time took his youth away*

For a while we toyed with an era, but later the era had no use for us

Later Zhang Yan's luck turned bad; he fell from favor and went to Shanghai

What a pity he lost his good looks, or who knows what heights he'd have reached

For me, thanks are due to life at the bottom, to ill luck and the Cultural Revolution

02:13, November 14, 2012. Seat 1A on Flight CA984 from Los Angeles to Beijing.

KINDHEARTED YANG LAN

Initially capitalists had the hardest time, because Chairman Mao hit them
    first, saying
"Capitalist roaders are still on the road; see the Cultural Revolution through
    to the end"
Her dad, Yang Yimu, was a high official in Ningxia: he was shamed and his
    house was searched
Yang Lan fell out of favor at school, and her family was in tough circumstances
They were evicted and had to live in a bungalow, but it was better than my
    house in the slum
She was nice to people, never judging us on the basis of wealth, so we got
    along with her
Once when I had nothing else to do, I knocked on her door, thinking I
    would lend her a book
Those children of privilege sitting around her said, "He's a thug, don't let
    him in"
That put Yang Lan in a bind; I told her I'd knocked on the wrong door and
    went away
For many years, deep down I even considered myself to be a hoodlum
Yang Lan's runny-nosed little brother Yang Quan used to get in fights
I would hold the enemy off so he could land a few more punches
When Yang Lan joined a production team, I found chances to chat with her
Later the reinstatement policies took effect; we were soon in different worlds
I hear that she retired and returned to her old home in Yinchuan
I hope to see her someday, have a good talk to help me deal with my regrets
I'll say, "I've done some thinking; now I know I'm a poet, not a thug"

02:49, November 14, 2012. Seat 1A on Flight CA984 from Los Angeles to Beijing.

PRETTY YANG XIAOFANG

Yang Xiaofang—if I got her name right[1]—was a bright, clever girl
Her father was an ace reporter; he climbed a crane to get some shots of
    Mongolian rodeo
For reasons that must remain undisclosed, I was a foot messenger for him
I really liked seeing her eyebrows arch in amazement over a good book
Thus I scoured heaven and earth to get a copy of *Anna Karenina* for her
My mother saw her and said, "She's quite a pretty young lady"
She moved with her father to Ningxia, then back to Beijing
Her father wrote and put up many posters during Cult-Revo
She probably knew that her father was called "the Mangy Dog"
I knew that he chased women shamelessly, but he always had a true love
She was a rich Ningxia wife known to all; he climbed over rooftops to get to
    her bedroom
Right then, Yang Xiaofang must have been in her room, crying over Anna
Time is for wringing one's hands over, most of all over Cult-Revo . . . there's
    no judging right or wrong
I don't know how her life turned out, but she comes to mind at times
On a visit home I met her on the street; she was serene, and I was timeworn
Her eyes brightened as if she wanted to talk; I was reserved and detached
Recalling it now, I blame myself; I feel a little bit regretful, a little bit sad

03:17, November 14, 2012. Seat 1A on Flight CA984 from Los Angeles to Beijing.

---

1. "Xiaofang" can be written 小芳 or 晓芳. The poet is not sure he has chosen the right homonym.

NA XIA'S MUSLIM BURIAL

We went to different middle schools, but we met at the poster wall
He was short but had nice calligraphy; many said that his posters were
    well-written
In arguments he was persuasive, but his relentless manner offended some
    adults
He would flap his arms and taunt, "How about it? Are you ready to rumble?"
During his sent-down days, he hiked with a red flag through the Liupan
    Mountains
That was the Red Army's route through Ningxia, and it set the whole
    province abuzz
In reality he mostly rode up mountains in one of the support vehicles
He was a hero whose reputation glowed red in that Worker-Peasant-Soldier
    era
As an exemplar for sent-down youth, he was always called to speak ahead
    of us
But I was more determined, vowing to sink lifelong roots in the countryside
Later he preceded me to Beijing as a student on the Worker-Peasant-Soldier
    Plan
He tested into a regular program, then stayed in Beijing to raise his kids
He also tested the waters of commerce, left his job, and started a company
Business was rough and he drank heavily, guzzling at night to fight insomnia
While hurrying home to see his sick mother, he suddenly died of hepatic
    edema
He was famous and he was somebody, so folks held a big Muslim funeral
    for him
Someone commented, "Half the imams in town came out, so his death was
    worth it"

03:51, November 14, 2012. Seat 1A on Flight CA984 from Los Angeles to Beijing.

LI HONGYU THE GOUT SUFFERER

During his youth in Ningxia, Li Hongyu was the son of a high official
His work-team days were short; I don't know how he took part in Cult-Revo
Many people in Ningxia say they knew him, which I have to wonder about
He is mild-tempered, likes history, claims he can shoot sparrows from 200
    meters
I get angry and say he's telling tales, because not even I have such good aim
He simply smiles, doesn't explain, and at the next meeting he'll brag again
Somehow he knows many Cult-Revo secrets, like who backstabbed whom
He also has a strong interest in the Qing dynasty, being descended from
    Manchu nobility
He is vice chairman of my company, but he works with painful slowness
When he does something he does it right, but I can't help blowing up at him
We both like eating sheep variety meats, but I go back to Yinchuan more often
Too bad his blood urea is high, and such goodies are restricted from his diet
When we reminisce about Cult-Revo, we always go over the battles . . . those
    corpses
He says he was bold . . . once at a morgue in a gym, he counted the bullet holes
He says one corpse's eyelids fluttered; then he chanted a mantra and it
    stopped
He agrees with my thinking that the Cultural Revolution will come again
But we will never be Chairman Mao's little red guards again

04:10, November 14, 2012. Seat 1A on Flight CA984 from Los Angeles to Beijing.

MY TEACHER TU YILING

Tu Yiling was my homeroom teacher and taught math in junior middle school
She was young then, and dreamy; her short frame seemed to dance when
    she walked
She would say, "Huang Yuping, straighten your back and walk right"
She organized critiques of me, but she was only going through the motions
When peasants led chore duty, if I sassed she'd say, "I'll stuff dirt in your
    mouth"
Once I slapped someone in class; she told me to get out of her classroom
I had ties to many book lovers, so she sometimes borrowed great works
    from me
That was underground activity: it was kept between heaven and us and no
    one else
She made my heart feel warm; she gave me days I can reminisce about
In my production team I couldn't sleep; one night I wrote her a long, loving
    letter
Looking back, it was an Oedipus complex and a sign of my youthful turmoil
When I saw her next, she still had that joyful laugh that drew me in
She often tells people, "When he was young, I knew he was going places"
She says that having a student like me makes her proud
I'll always remember being fond of her dark, damp house
Boy students would pour out their troubles, and girls would reveal who
    liked whom
That was a different Cult-Revo; that was a different track of existence

04:33, November 14, 2012. Seat 1A on Flight CA984 from Los Angeles to Beijing.

THE POET QIN KEWEN

He was our language teacher, but he always taught class in Ningxia dialect
When he read a poem about a peasant uprising, white foam would fleck
    his lips
He seemed unaware of Cult-Revo's coming—he continued to write all
    kinds of poems
Because of him, the *Ningxia Daily* published a poem of mine when I was
    thirteen
He never concerned himself with the critiques or punishments I suffered
He would sit at his desk revising my poems, as if he were tackling a major
    matter
During "Criticize Confucius," he would knit his brows and fix my pomposities
In those revolutionary times we put fervor into our lines, to shake heaven
    and earth
After I was sent down, he was the culture editor at the *Ningxia Daily*, so he
    made room for my poems
I was sent to Peking U by the *Daily*, under the Worker-Peasant-Soldier Plan
Once the *Guangming Daily* published a suite of his poems in praise of his
    teachers
That created a stir in Ningxia: it was an event that made our frontier city proud
I always wanted to ask him why secrets about him were not spread on posters
Why wasn't he critiqued or made to critique people?
Now I'm doing all right: As the poet Luo Ying, I send him my published
    collections
He doesn't write new-style poems; he heads the Shi-ci Association and uses
    the old forms
Maybe he is nostalgic for old things, but I'm sure he's no fan of the Cultural
    Revolution

05:11, November 14, 2012. Seat 1A on Flight CA984 from Los Angeles to Beijing.

DUAN ZHONGREN, "THE MANGY DOG"

Being called "mangy" back then was nothing: looking back from today, we
    were all "mangy"
For the love of a rich woman, Duan moved from Beijing to this frontier city
He seemed to live for this, though the scandal took on stormlike proportions
He wrote big-character posters attacking anyone who called him "Mangy
    Dog"
He was a reporter with a good camera and a good daughter named Xiaofang
He lived with grit and valor, and people dared not trifle with him
It was a scoundrelly era, and you had to be a scoundrel to live well
Thanks to Cult-Revo, a generation turned scoundrel and tore into each other
Duan Zhongren's posters stayed up for three days before someone dared
    cover them
No rebels dared to point a gun at his head out of meanness
The city knew where he climbed at night, and how his ribs got broken
Roofs of cottages went unrepaired back then; he fell through onto
    someone's bed
He dusted himself off, said he was "sleepwalking," then went to a hospital
    for painkillers
His posters were not seen for months, so the city could sigh with relief
Once my reputation was made, I wanted to see him, in my role as section chief
No one knows if he's still alive, or if he's staying healthy in retirement
What conclusion could be more fitting to such an absurd era?

05:26, November 14, 2012. Seat 1A on Flight CA984 from Los Angeles to Beijing.

AN AMIABLE FRIEND NAMED HUA XINHE

Because of Cult-Revo, fallen power holders had to get along with hoodlums
I am grateful to Hua Xinhe: he was kind to me, though he was a high
    cadre's son
He gave me slices of sausage—I had never tasted that kind of meat before
So I didn't complain when he borrowed my big dictionary and kept it
As a direct target of the revolution, he was closer to the bottom than I
When red guards ransacked his house, I shot pellets at them from the roof
He never mentioned his father, who was locked up in jail
I forget whether he was also taken under guard to watch his father's shaming
After Cult-Revo, his father was pardoned and became a national leader
Later I saw Xinhe in Beijing; after a few drinks, he recalled who I was
He said he was retired, doing some drinking while working on a project
After many drinks, he patted my cheek and said, "Good going, Little Huang!"
I knew his father was in power during the "Two Antis," when many people
    died
As they used to say, the blood debt for my father's death lies with Hua's family
But I like him anyway, because in that era you were not in command of
    yourself
We were all victims and violators: you couldn't say what was fair or not
I curse that era for happening, just as I curse the time when it will come again

05:56, November 14, 2012. Seat 1A on Flight CA984 from Los Angeles to Beijing.

SPECIAL-ENTRY STUDENTS AT PEKING UNIVERSITY

Admitted in '77, we were the last group under the Worker-Peasant-Soldier
  Plan; we didn't really know where we fit in
Workers on campus would yell, *Run them over: those are Worker-Peasant-
  Soldier students!*
We went to class, but newspapers said we were a lost, useless generation
Yet Cult-Revo was still going on in society, because the appetite for struggle
  was still keen
We needed dissension, so altercations broke out in crowds, and students
  formed factions
Beijinger, provincial, military, local, urban, and rural—no one deferred to
  anyone
I think the armed strife must have ended too soon, before we got it out of
  our system
China has never lacked for rabble-rousers, and its hell has always been other
  people
Yi Liangbing came as a worker, then rose to become chair of the Chinese
  Department, but we shamed him for his ties to the Gang of Four
I took charge of shouting slogans—*Yi Liangbing must lower his head and
  admit guilt!*
That struggle session gave us passion and release—those are Cult-Revo traits
We all had a lot to answer for, because we were the cream of Cult-Revo,
  which was why we were sent to Beijing on the Plan
Many of our classmates had come to Peking U because their reinstated
  parents had connections
Capitalist roaders were still on the road, but Cult-Revo had ended: we had
  wakened from the Worker-Peasant-Soldier dream
Children cast off by our own era, when the revolution was won we were
  cast off yet again
Some were resentful, some indignant, some felt chagrin, but we all balled
  our fists
We had all been red guards, and the worst thing that could happen would
  be to have another Cultural Revolution

18:19, November 14, 2012. Bench at Xigu Fishing Ground, Beijing Kunlun Hotel.

DUAN LEI'S DEATH

Duan Lei was on the Inner Mongolian Wrestling Team; he wrote well, and
his stories were enthralling
He would stand by the wall holding a bottle, watching his girlfriend dance
with others
He and I came from the Northwest; we shared a sense of frontier justice
and felt simpatico
We were accomplished in navigating the currents of factional strife and
skeptical of everyone
At mealtimes in the cafeteria, our '77 and '78 classmates liked to cut in line
People thought the special-entry students were a notch below and wanted
us chased off campus
I took charge of pulling students from the line, and Duan Lei knocked them
off their feet
Cult-Revo turned us into wolves, and we could not change our wolfishness
easily
The Beijing special-entry students plotted to boycott the lead teacher's
classes, because she didn't like high cadres' children
Duan Lei and I kicked down their dorm doors and cursed their forebears
for eighteen generations
I don't know if that was in the May 4th tradition, because *my* nationality
had been smashing everything for a century
I don't know if that was the New Culture Movement, because *my*
nationality had overthrown Confucius a century earlier
In my college years, the water in No-Name Lake was limpid, but our bodies
were still dusted with cornmeal
In my college years, Cult-Revo wound to a close, because the last group of
special-entry students graduated
Duan Lei went back to Inner Mongolia, but his work at the TV station
made him bad-tempered and melancholy
Once on New Year's I paid a visit to remember old times; we drank and
talked about Stalin and Lu Xun
Late that night Duan Lei died suddenly; no one had told me his kidneys
were bad and he shouldn't have been drinking

03:03, November 15, 2012. Changhe-wan in Beijing.

BUILDING 26

Building 26 was for male international students, and 25 was for females;
    I've heard they're being torn down
As a student-tutor, I shared a dorm room with Hjorleifur from Iceland
I could sleep in late, but I was often asked if So-and-So from such-and-such
    a country was doing anything wrong
I thought Cult-Revo had ended, but our adversarial thinking was still
    deep-seated
There were many Palestinian students—they made lots of trouble, mostly
    by chasing girls
"Reform and Opening" was underway, and Chinese girls were fascinated by
    any male who could be called *Laowai* ["foreigner"]
One night I helped the school office block a Chinese woman in a room with
    Hussein from Palestine
At dawn Public Security took her away, and I heard she was given a
    multiyear sentence
Another girl would sit on Hussein's bed, sewing bedcovers and clothes for him
She would give me disdainful looks as if to say, "Beat it, you Chinese mud
    turtle"
Albanians liked to trade foreign exchange and run off to Hong Kong for
    clothes to sell
North Korean students were mysterious and stiffly formal, always wearing a
    Kim Il-sung medal
Black students had ways of bringing in Sony cassette players, which they
    sold for a good price
Hjorleifur would bring a golden-haired chick over, and ask me to go
    somewhere else
We never let the international students out of our sight; I was well aware of
    the complexity of struggles with the enemy
We guarded against ourselves, against outsiders, against friends and
    enemies, against the past and the present and even the future
We had worn armbands and badges, stood against Soviet revisionists and
    American imperialists, and we had just done away with the Gang of Four

03:32, November 15, 2012. Changhe-wan in Beijing.

BUILDING 15 IN DIAOYUTAI COMPOUND

Diaoyutai was where Wang Hongwen[1] liked to shoot crows: they're so
    numerous that they blot out the sun . . .
Jiang Qing had secluded herself behind curtains in Building 15, pacing and
    brooding about Cult-Revo's future
After going to work for the Central Propaganda Ministry, I read cadres' files
    and issued transfers from Building 15
Mostly to carry out the reinstatement policy and bring sent-down cadres
    from farms back to work at Central Propaganda
With all those people, the crows cawed restlessly and dropped shit on our
    heads
With all those people, the agenda overflowed with questions of political
    outlook, clashing lines, and Cult-Revo grudges
Li Quan was the first to join a rebel faction: he critiqued Lu Dingyyi,
    shamed Zhou Yang, and opposed Hu Yaobang
Now he denies it, says he was victimized, and lets it slip that Liu Zhe was
    close with Jiang Qing's hired pens
Ye Mei wrote to Jiang Qing in praise of model operas, said they pointed to a
    new century of proletarian culture, but now she won't admit it
Wang Min, who was in a different faction from hers, organized people to
    report on her activities during Cult-Revo
Cai Ying is Literature and Arts Bureau chief, but when he went back to
    work, someone told on him for denying that art comes from life
Qin Zhou says he must mention the dictatorship of proles, because it is a
    brilliant theory of Marxism-Leninism
They all hate the Gang of Four, and now they can all breathe easy
They all claim to be victims of Cult-Revo, and say the blame should be laid
    on the Gang of Four
But I read through their files and know that they've all been harried and
    harrying each other in these movements
They've all reported on others and written letters of loyalty; they've all
    conducted revolution within their own souls
I work in Building 15 of Diaoyutai Compound; of course we don't wear red
    armbands or wave *Quotations of Chairman Mao* anymore

04:17, November 15, 2012. Changhe-wan in Beijing.

---

1. Wang Hongwen (1935–1996) attracted Mao Zedong's attention in the late sixties as the
leader of a red guard rebel faction in Shanghai. He was brought into the Central Committee
by Mao in 1969 and became a member of the Gang of Four in 1974.

THE MOVEMENT TO CLEANSE SPIRITUAL POLLUTION

Old Zhou Yang regrets all the persecutions, the ultra-leftism and movement
politics; now he wants to restore normal order
He says we should reread and reconceive "Talks at the Yan'an Forum on
Literature"
He also brought up human alienation, which sparked outrage and led some
to declare "Cleansing of Spiritual Pollution"
Back again to the battleground of critique, so people can step forward along
familiar lines and say incisive things
Everyone seizes the historical opportunity, divides into interest groups that
in truth are clashing sides—closed off to each other
When Li Honglin was forced to do a self-examination, Dai Zhen got up
shouting, "Revolution is not a matter of mild, yielding virtues"
Li Fu committed suicide in Hainan, because he was considered a traitor to
Marxism-Leninism and Mao Zedong Thought
We couldn't put up posters, but our pens flew to promote our clashing views
They all claimed to be the most revolutionary and selfless, like rebel factions
that were always right
They all agreed we can't stir up another political movement, but lines of
thought have to be clearly drawn
We bought food in the same cafeteria, but at our desks we were locked in a
contest of wills
Because Gu Xiang wrote an essay on alienation, he had to walk down the
hall with his head lowered
Those who critiqued him held their heads high, almost like red guards
ready to spread-eagle him
Because Zhou Yang went around saying, "I'm sorry," some said he was
putting on a political show
Others remembered his purges and diatribes with animosity that would last
forever
After Cult-Revo, he woke up: some have broken free, but historical
accounts must be settled
But that would be using a movement to purge a movement, trading one
critique for another critique

05:03, November 15, 2012. Changhe-wan in Beijing.

ZHOU YI'S SPUTUM

Zhou Yi was a veteran of Central Propaganda; during Cult-Revo he was
    sent to a farm in Jiangxi
When he and his family left, no one saw them off, for he had plotted the
    downfall of many
He came back due to the reinstatements, and still no one went to meet him
He was made office director, a squat, loud-voiced man with bloodhound
    features
He had harmed people and so become a victim; then he wanted to harm
    people even more
He yelled at me loudly, which was his way of telling people he was back in
    power
He said that Cult-Revo had been hard on him, and he still recalled who had
    written posters about him
He would adamantly say that historical accounts must be settled
But they had all come through Cult-Revo; all of them had written down
    what he said
Such as when he was unhappy with what ideas, or when he had
    disrespected a driver
Such as his dissolute ways, having that girl from the Admin Section bathe
    naked in his office
Poor old Zhou Yi's temper flared as his body grew frail; he was eager to take
    revenge but left himself vulnerable to return fire
He never made vice minister; in a hopeless mood he retired, and no one
    shook his hand
He lived downstairs from me; I saw him every day in the yard, watching
    pets in the sunlight
When women walked by he would stare at their breasts, not caring about
    their offended looks
I ventured into business, had some money and a car, but he simply spat at
    the sight of me
Later he died, and I attribute that to the hatred he had harbored for others
    since Cult-Revo

05:23, November 15, 2012. Changhe-wan in Beijing.

A WORN SLIPPER NAMED XIA ZUNBEI

She was Party secretary in a public agency, but she wore a cheerless
    expression, as if she lived to purge people
During Cult-Revo she had been paraded through the streets with worn
    shoes hanging from her neck
The rebels had spread-eagled her and harried her for sleeping with men and
    taking the capitalist line
She spoke of the past with glowering eyes, balling her fists and shaking
In her eyes all young people belonged to a rebel faction, so she spoke in icy
    tones
People in her age group had collected incriminating materials against her,
    so she wouldn't spend time with them
She disliked me the most, because sometimes I let my disdain and wildness
    show
Thus I harbored contempt for her; I would whisper to others about bad
    things she'd done
Cult-Revo had tempered me into an iron fighter, in the habit of mutual strife
The ravages of Cult-Revo had made her hostile; she was wary of others and
    keen on persecuting them
She would comment coldly on my faults, so I wouldn't be given responsible
    posts
I had support from her rivals; they filled me in on her political stance and
    whose office she spent too much time in
She did not outlast me: she retired, and I didn't have to see her again
Hearing that she was gravely ill, I gleefully wished her an early death
All who stand against us will fall—this was our law of struggle in the Cultural
    Revolution
If you don't look out for yourself, heaven will destroy you—this was what
    passed for truth during Cult-Revo
Thus I would agree that everyone is a Huang Nubo; everyone is a Xia Zunbei

    08:43, November 17, 2012 Seat 11A on Flight CA1501 to Shanghai.

THE SHREWISHNESS OF GE LEI

Ge Lei was the Vice Bureau chief directly over me; we all kept out of her
    way because of her shrewishness
During Cult-Revo she was in a rebel faction; she had an uncanny knack for
    standing on the right side
She was wary of others, and her distrust of them was fated to come back
    around
For instance, she furtively went through the minister's desk and the
    secretary's drawers, looking for secrets
She did not admit to writing posters and unsigned letters or those statements
    of loyalty to Jiang Qing
The Cult-Revo Sweep-Up Group reluctantly let her pass, and she was put in
    charge of external propaganda funds
When she wore that fake smile, we knew that one of her "revolutionary
    acts" was coming
She might hint that it was highly likely X was a follower of a frowned-upon
    line
She never admitted her affair with another Vice Bureau chief, but they went
    around like a couple
Some say that in Cult-Revo she critiqued her husband, so they acted like
    total strangers
She would wail and make scenes in the minister's office, scaring the old guy
    so much he'd approve anything
She used external propaganda funds on gifts or activities for leaders' children
She had money and power, so her son was the first to study overseas
In members' meetings she criticized young people for dreaming about
    overseas study, saying they should be content with their work
Cult-Revo made us two-faced: we were all harmed by it, but we also
    benefited from it
Our game rules were to speak two different ways, be two kinds of people,
    and take advantage of both sides
Ge Lei may still be alive because she went through the Cultural Revolution

05:45, November 15, 2012. Changhe-wan in Beijing.

A BURGLAR SECTION CHIEF IN THE CENTRAL PROPAGANDA MINISTRY

The house of the army orchestra's leader was burglarized; cash and watches
    were missing
Because I'd gone for dinner to a nearby house, they reported me as a suspect
Although I was a vice section chief at Central Propaganda, the ministry's
    leaders and Public Security used a major operation to arrest me
I figured that everyone who went through Cult-Revo became suspicious, so
    the organization would not believe them without good reason
Cong Shen was my underling; he stealthily riffled through my files and
    dusted for fingerprints
The old section chief, Wu Jing, looked alarmed—his eyes would follow me,
    then turn away
The police station brought carloads of witnesses to identify me from behind
    a screen
The all nodded, said they'd seen me on a motorbike, or even walking on a roof
They tricked me into going to the police station to be fingerprinted; when
    they questioned me harshly, I wanted to throw a glass in a policeman's face
I was disturbed that they made me out to be a burglar—a former
    militiaman who had arrested no-goodniks and was a section-level cadre
    at Central Propaganda
I was saddened—because my activities that day were clear, yet nobody
    checked the record of the meeting I'd gone to at the ministry
To live in a nation where you may meet with a sudden reversal at any moment,
    with nowhere to seek redress—this is surely a Cult-Revo syndrome
When the truth came to light, I showed my red guard colors by making a
    scene at the police station, breaking glass and kicking a door
I went to the army orchestra leader's compound, where I ranted and raved
    about them on the street like a hysterical low-class woman
At work, I berated people until my voice was hoarse; I abused them in
    veiled terms
The office was like an ice cellar: we wore blank looks and walked around as
    if on eggshells
We are a Cult-Revo nation, and Cult-Revo people have no reason to expect
    that other people will trust them

08:11, November 17, 2012. Gate L01, Terminal 3 at Beijing Airport.

ZHU BING AT OUR PUBLISHING HOUSE

The nineties had come, but Zhu Bing still did things the red guard way,
daring to take the offensive
He led the way in selling off ISBNs; he had a do-or-die group that could
squeeze or push as needed, ready for "civil assault and martial defense"
He would send beautiful women to seduce the Press's directors, then force
them to approve publication numbers
They would even go over the walls at night, delivering scandalous
documents about the director to higher-ups
Zhu made no secret of his past as a red guard leader, for that was a thrilling
time of his life
Now, due to "Reform and Opening," he intended to live it fully and swim in
it like a duck
As the new vice director at the Press, I wanted to earn merit by operating
honestly and putting out good books
He vowed that he would run me out within a year, so as not to block
everyone's path to riches
He said, "In Cult-Revo we flirted with death and let our youth go to waste,
with nothing to show for it
If you won't let us improve our lives, don't expect your own life to be easy"
They forgot that I had come up as a little red guard, and I knew the survival
strategies of hoodlum proles
Overnight I struck all their names off the roll and stopped their pay
They wrote on the pavement *Down with Huang Nubo*, and they went to
accuse me at the controlling ministry
They mobilized a mass of people to say I had whored and embezzled and
had connections to the fallen mayor Chen Xitong
While they mailed their accusatory letters in all directions, I opposed them
with an organizational decision
I voluntarily sent a self-examination to my leaders, saying I had handled this
too roughly and would be more careful the next time
Victory goes to the valiant: Zhu Bing treated me to dumplings and admitted
defeat before leaving

06:07, November 15, 2012. Changhe-wan in Beijing.

LIU QUANXING'S BATTLE

As an old red guard, Liu Quanxing set up his own camp in the publishing
house
He never provoked anyone, but no one was allowed to question his
consignments
He was seemingly traumatized by Cult-Revo; he was dispirited and would
say, "Being a red guard was a total disaster"
He earned money under the table and drank sake, which he viewed as some
kind of restitution for Cult-Revo
He admitted that in Cult-Revo he had ransacked central leaders' houses,
and Mao Zedong had received him at Tiananmen
His head had been gashed open, and he had the bloodied army cap and
armband to prove it
He said, "You and I should get along peacefully: let me live my life and
don't upset the applecart"
He said, "You fill your post as press director, and I'll sell my consignments:
we won't interfere with each other"
I joked about his bandit-like panache, but reminded him that I had joined
a rural work team and had gotten inside the red wall, so my struggle
mentality was pretty intense
I suspended him and inventoried the book depository; I also ordered that
his little vault be opened
Liu the old red guard returned to battle: he gathered a crowd of petitioners
who demanded that our press be occupied by a working group
He said, "I'll see to it that you're smeared with mud and your good name is
ruined"
The working team wanted *me* to account for the stolen ISBNs *I* had
supposedly sold and the excess editing fees *I* had taken
They critiqued me for reviling people with terrible language unsuited to a
leading cadre
My will to struggle was keen, and I met the attacks with composure; I
struck a balance between substance and implication, living up to my
background as a little red guard
Three days after the working team pulled out, I ordered Liu off the premises
Later he drank to excess and died of liver cancer; on his deathbed he said,
"Huang Nubo is not a bad guy"

06:27, November 15, 2012. Changhe-wan in Beijing.

A SLICK CHARACTER NAMED WU SHIMIN

That slick character was not easy to deal with, so I brought him into the
    Press's Party Committee
I knew that a sweep-up team had purged him from the Xi'an Army
    Languages Institute because he had led a rebel faction
He came early and left late, always pacing the halls, but I never knew what
    he was up to
He office cleared three million characters a day, making my stomach churn
    with worry over too many mistakes
He wanted to publish a biography of Hitler that would make big money and
    make the Press famous
He assigned people to record my every word and deed, copying all my
    written comments
His driver conducted surveillance and reported everyone I'd seen and
    everyone I'd railed at
He wanted to know whom I'd make trouble for next, whose post would be
    cut when I adjusted the lineup
He stood at my door to comfort the people I'd yelled at, saying I was crude
    and that I had no respect for people
I thought to myself: he foresees that I will butt heads with him and wants to
    stop it before it gets to that point
When I purged him, he refused to let his file be transferred out, on the
    strength of his Party membership
I gave the office strict orders to mail his file to his neighborhood committee,
    which resulted in its being lost without a trace
Then he could not seek employment, so he went around creating
    disorderly scenes
The Cadre Affairs Office wrote a report, saying that my treatment of the
    matter was not in accord with organizational rules
But this was simply the battle mode of a Cult-Revo fighter, not to be afraid
    of anyone
The price I paid was making the organization unhappy with me; the price
    he paid was being set adrift in life
To sum it up, the little red guard showed gall out of proportion to his size,
    and the slick old rebel was thrown from his horse

06:43, November 15, 2012. Changhe-wan in Beijing.

THE NEW PRESS DIRECTOR, WANG LI

Due to all the stratagems in my head, for a while I thought I was a bad person

When the new director came, I knew that my exit would not be graceful: it would be a struggle

He had been a problem for the minister of construction, so he was foisted upon our press

Of course the minister was fed up with me by then, because lots of people had come forward with grievances

The vice chair forwarded grievance letters with the comment "Check into what kind of person he is"

So the minister gave the nod for Wang Li to supersede me, to see what I had up my sleeve

Wang Li had just been deprived of an adversary and was coming to a new battleground

Most of my underlings defected to him, judging that my ascendancy had passed

Being a lone wolf with nowhere to go, I steeled myself for a fight to the finish

Tragedy was my lot in life because I went through Cult-Revo and had to join the red guard

I gathered evidence of his activities, such as making out with the accountant soon after his arrival

I said that in meetings he had disparaged the minister as a mediocre talent

I found his adversaries, who told me he had met with Zhang Chunqiao

In his writings he had beaten the drum for the Gang of Four's bandwagon

No one believed me outright, but they didn't completely discount me

The organization approved my plan to split the Press off, so I could catch my breath

From then on I stopped believing that the Cultural Revolution had ended

07:00, November 15, 2012. Changhe-wan in Beijing.

PERSONNEL CHIEF ZHUO WEN

As chief of a ministry-level agency, Young Zhuo was close to my age, but he
took a dim view of me

Speaking for the investigation team, he concluded that my working style
was harsh and disrespectful

He said the Press's conflicts had arisen due to my narrow-mindedness

He criticized me for firing people at will, not considering the future
prospects of old and young comrades

He treated the Press's accountant to late dinners of lamb hotpot, pumping
her for info

She was a beauty with a beaked nose who had gone over to Wang Li, the
new press director

His wife, who was filing for divorce for infidelity, had been trailing him

She noticed Zhuo Wen booking a room with a female underling from his
section

Unhappy with Zhuo Wen, I hatched a secret plan, asking his wife and the
accountant's husband to come forward

This is a consummate Cult-Revo move that never fails to devastate the enemy

Zhuo Wen claimed that I'd arrived on the scene arrogantly from Central
Propaganda, causing instability at the Press

He said I had purged the dissenting camp so that I could take the Press over
for personal gain

He said that the Press is a key cultural front and should be in the stewardship
of someone politically reliable

He wrote a report and asked me out for drinks, to tell me what "nice things"
he'd said about me

Then he showed me reams of grievance letters, wanting to see if I'd be
outraged

I paid the tab and chuckled: "Your wife and the accountant's hubby went to
the ministry today to air your dirty laundry"

He laughed and said, "Touché"—It's a basic Cult-Revo skill to make each
move more ruthless than the last

09:12, November 16, 2012. Changhe-wan in Beijing.

THE PRESS THAT CAME BACK TO LIFE

ISBNs were a monopoly item that enabled the Press to survive
As the boss at the Press, I put a stranglehold on certain people's path to
    wealth, so they wanted to strangle me
They covertly gathered materials so damning that the higher-ups ordered
    the Press to cease operations
This was big news in the nineties, known to everyone in the country
I had been a hoodlum in my youth, and in adulthood I was not an "oil-
    saving lamp"[1]
Facing ill-wishers near and far brought out the fighter in me—at last I could
    be a red guard for a while
In the open I filed a suit in court; under cover I searched for info on top-
    down collusion
By day I hot-headedly fired people; by night I penned sensational reports to
    expose offenses
Rumors need not be backed up fully: a little fishing in murky waters always
    turns up something
People wiped themselves as soon as possible after taking a shit, so the
    leaders didn't know whom to believe
On the basis of the "Administrative Tort Law" enacted after Reform and
    Opening, the judge ruled in my favor
I was helped by the "see-it-through-to-the-end" courage I had learned as a
    Cult-Revo rebel
After privately handing the verdict to media friends, I went to my hometown
    and drank for three days
Thanks to Cult-Revo for training me, and thanks to my hometown for
    letting a little red guard grow up to adulthood
Amid a worldwide stir, the department above us paid the 40 yuan fee for
    filing my lawsuit
The Press revived and the bad guys were purged; I was a good guy again
    with lots of prestige
Later someone told me the Press had been a private money box for an even
    higher leader's daughter

02:07, November 16, 2012. Changhe-wan in Beijing.

---

1. An oil-saving lamp burns so little oil that it provides only a dim glow. When this common
idiom is used to describe a person, it means that he or she is deferential and does not like to
make waves. By saying that he was "not an 'oil-saving lamp,'" Luo Ying is saying that he did
not mind stirring things up and would not back down from a fight.

MINISTER XIE'S CAUTIOUS USE OF UNDERLINGS

People relegated to the back bench often become heads of associations or
    societies
They must behave politely, but deep down they are filled with
    dissatisfaction and suspicion
Minister Xie used to listen with half-closed eyes as I reported on the
    problems I dealt with
He loved tennis, so I had to find five-star hotels with courts and quietly pay
    the fee
He often switched coaches and never asked the price; he also wanted me to
    find people to play doubles
The reforms went further, so the time came to leave that job and test the
    business waters
Because he had said we were not permitted to use public assets for our own
    personal gain
On the tenth anniversary of my enterprise, I put on a variety show with
    models at the Beijing Hotel
At home he spent a sleepless night writing down questions to pass around
    at the ministry
He said, "We need to find out how Huang Nubo got so big, because he may
    owe a share of his assets to the Association"
He told his son to set up an enterprise, saying that the only way to make big
    money is to master some kind of shady gimmick
I went to pay him a New Year's visit, chatting and catching up just as
    humbly as ever
I told him I'd gotten on the Forbes list thanks to his approval when I gave
    up my iron rice bowl
He said that creditors were blocking his son's door; I promised to help with
    this in good time
He thought for a moment and told me he was not the one who had said,
    "Huang Nubo should be used with caution"
He is right: For people who lived through Cult-Revo, it's no use trying to
    figure out who's a human and who's a ghoul

09:51, November 17, 2012. Changhe-wan in Beijing.

THE RED GUARD GENE

If you've been a red guard, your way of doing things seems to proclaim,
    "Who dares to mess with me?" . . .
For instance, if someone steps on your foot, you step on his foot three times
    in return
For instance, if someone stares at you, you stare right back
When your eyes can shoot such daggers, who needs to hurl those "national
    curse words"?
For instance, while ascending a mountain, I feel an urge to whack a certain
    climber with my staff because he pisses and clears his sinuses behind
    my tent
The night before summiting Aconcagua, Russians drank and sang at the
    advance camp
My malice drove me to grab a rock, ready to smash someone's head
My reckless tantrum scared them into moving their tent in the dark
I jumped and howled like a crazed dog, not giving an inch at 6,100 meters
Coming off the summit, I was still simmering and ready to clobber anyone
    in my path
Climbers averted their eyes and looked downward, thinking I had water on
    the brain
When we said our goodbyes, the Argentine guide asked what had made me
    so furious
He said on the mountain we must not hold things against people, because
    being intolerant is not a good way to get back down alive
I had no answer—just said it might have been due to mountain sickness
In fact, I think Cult-Revo changed our state of being—so everyone is the
    Big Honcho
Or let's say everyone has been damaged, so they claim the right to damage
    others

02:38, November 16, 2012. Changhe-wan in Beijing.

HOODLUM SYNDROME

During the twenty-first-century Internet era, an anonymous letter is a
    newsworthy oddity
It makes you suspect that the letter was sent straight from the Cultural
    Revolution
A few poets wanted to wield power in matters of Chinese poetry, presiding
    over its entry into the world
In standard Cult-Revo mode, they exposed the bad guys in the poetic ranks
They said having an army poet as our group's vice pres is like an armed
    takeover
They said one vice pres is unclean, visiting whores and making money
    corruptly
They said one vice pres sullied our group by buying his way into office
Lots of bosses can write poetry that is better than his doggerel
Nothing need be done about an unsigned letter delivered to poets
    nationwide
Killing a person may not take bullets—we've done such things in Cult-Revo
Who was behind the unsigned letter is no mystery—heaven and earth and
    you and I know
This is a rule of the game—the hoodlum syndrome of our Chinese nationality
Since we smashed everything once, the syndrome makes us go on smashing
The twenty-first century hasn't been able to cleanse us or turn everyone's
    thoughts toward the good
The anonymous letter faded away in a manner befitting its origins
Because "Anonymous" once waved the Red Book, wore an armband, and
    had a close brush with death
At our conference, "Anonymous" and his targets exchanged smiles and
    waves of acknowledgment

03:03, November 16, 2012. Changhe-wan in Beijing.

A DEVIANT ERA

If someone has worn a red armband and been a red guard, he will have what
  it takes to succeed in this world
If he once joined a production team and a militia unit, he will have what it
  takes to make a fortune in business
If two such people go head to head in the corporate arena, it will be a fight
  to the death
Such a business battle will be a heart-pounding drama, a lowdown brawl
We've been honchos and now we're both the Big Honcho, so if the deal
  sours, we'll lay our lives on the line to win
Take a certain man who was my friend when we did joint projects, but who
  is now in close combat with me
He said I owed him money, I said he cut corners on workmanship, and each
  complaint was voiced more loudly than the last
He bought off a judge, I marshaled evidence, and each move was more
  ruthless than the one before
He was going to hold a press conference, so I prepared reams of material
He secretly paid the mob for protection, so I gauged his moves and did not
  take them lightly
We kept up proper appearances, speaking out of both sides of our mouths,
  while watching for the coup de grâce
We were former rebels, so we were not likely to play a predictable card game
If a nationality takes a deviant road, it will have a deviant generation
Though we wear Western suits and ties, we cannot purge that deviant gene
We know this will not bankrupt either of us, but we want to see who blinks
  first
Wealth could not make us high-minded, because of how we got our start
Here we are in the twenty-first century, settling conflicts the red guard way

03:28, November 16, 2012. Changhe-wan in Beijing.

BIG HONCHO STYLE

We Chinese are all honchos, due to going through the Cultural Revolution
For instance, as a condo owner I am the honcho, and you'd better do my
    bidding or I won't pay the property fee
For instance, water leaked into my condo, but I won't let anyone fix it or pay
    damages because I want to make a scene
The basic story goes—if you make me unhappy, I won't give you a
    moment's rest
For instance, if family members can't get in the main gate, I'll throw a tantrum
Yet I complained just last night because a stranger rang my bell and gave me
    a fright
Hell is other people, neighbors are the enemy, and couples are sitting
    ducks—ever since Cult-Revo
Being well-off doesn't stop my body from filling with rancor if someone's
    will opposes mine
Li Dongqiang has three luxury condos but never pays the fee, because
    property management smashed in his door
Thus he vowed to organize an owners' committee in order to kick out the
    property management company in revenge
He sent out e-mails and went to the neighborhood committee to accuse the
    manager of thuggery
Property management scratched his car, banged on his door, and berated
    him at his workplace
I see so many people fighting, playing the honcho, still wearing red
    armbands and being red guards
After becoming director, Li fired the property manager and then resigned
    the same day, because he had gotten what he wanted
A different Li strove to become chairman, because some people's dogs went
    missing after a new manager came in
The new property manager cut off his power and water, vowing not to let
    him get off easy
You see, we are all honchos; we are all the law of the land; a mentality of
    strife is our national trait in the twenty-first century

03:55, November 16, 2012. Changhe-wan in Beijing.

EREHWON

The memory of a nationality cannot be erased, so people begin to reminisce
   about the Great Proletarian Cultural Revolution
We miss those life-or-death thrills, those kneeling officials, those ransacked
   houses and rich folks dragged off without mercy
People made snappy gestures of greeting that sliced the air briskly, like Ah
   Q showing he belonged to the revolutionary camp[1]
On the Web people go to "Erehwon" to post mourning verses for the Gang
   of Four or fond memories of Jiang Qing
Ma Licheng talks about eight currents of thought that link back to the class
   struggle[2]
Now that my name is on the Forbes list, will I bring calamity upon myself?
Thinking of my home being ransacked, of being paraded through the
   streets, of being reduced to ruin and poverty, I have to laugh
I am worrying about the same kind of resentment and rebellion and
   ruthlessness I showed then
Things have gone one way for a while, and it may be time for us Chinese to
   swing the other way
With Cult-Revo over and no struggles in sight, where do we get our kicks in
   life?
Yet I know that Erehwon is not so ethereal as to be untainted by any speck
   of dust
Behind one triumphant general are thousands of bare bones, and our
   nationality needs lots of red guards to charge into the fray
I know about those eight currents of thought—they all try to rewrite history
A portion of the people were allowed to get rich first, so maybe they should
   be the first to be done away with

---

1. Ah Q was the protagonist of *The True Story of Ah Q* by Lu Xun (1881–1936). Published in
1921, this novella was perhaps the first work of modern fiction written in vernacular Chinese.
It describes the self-deluding adventures of a would-be arriviste whose egoism hinders his
adjustment to a changing society during China's Xinhai Revolution. Seeing that revolution-
aries were becoming leaders in society, Ah Q imagined himself to be one of them and tried
to join their ranks. Because he had done nothing worthy of notice, he could not gain their
attention.
2. Ma Licheng's book *Dangdai Zhongguo bazhong shehui sichao* (Eight Currents of Social
Thought in Contemporary China) was published in 2012 by Shehui Kexue Wenxian Chu-
banshe (Social Science Documents Press). In this book and in related essays, Ma expounds
on eight currents of thought that are interlocked in a way that causes the same issues to
emerge again and again. As described by Ma, they can be summarized under the following
rubrics: 1) mainstream thinking; 2) old leftism; 3) new leftism; 4) social democratic think-
ing; 5) liberalism; 6) nationalist thinking; 7) national essentialism (with an emphasis on
populist egalitarianism); 8) New Confucianism.

I get up at night looking for my armband in the moonlight, to see if it is still
  red
In the mirror my complexion is bloodless; my gaze is deadpan, resembling
  neither a revolutionary nor a poor person
In Erehwon am I a callously rich target of the revolution, or am I a red guard
  with bulging pockets?

04:37, November 16, 2012. Changhe-wan in Beijing.

SINGING RED SONGS

Teresa Teng's death was no great loss, for I'd had my fill of her decadent
  crooning
I have heard that she was a KMT spy, so she never sang red songs
As for me, from early years I could sing "Cruising on the Sea Relies on the
  Helmsman"
I heard red songs while sleeping; I heard them while getting out of bed
That is why we could see the Proletarian Cultural Revolution through to the
  end
The red songs of an era nurtured the red guards of an era
In the twenty-first century, red songs resounded anew in the Great Hall of
  the People
Those days I'd forgotten . . . my revolutionary youth . . . came clearly to mind
Red Army clothes, flags held up by red sisters, brightly colored pumpkins in
  Naniwan
I guessed that after intermission they would play "The Great Proletarian
  Cultural Revolution Is Fine"
I did not stay for the second half, but my heart leapt at the thought
Some died because of Cult-Revo; some won fame and fortune because of it;
  some were condemned by it to hell
The armbands worn by singers of red songs are as red as those the red
  guards wore
The heart of one who sings red songs holds the same passion as a red
  guard's heart
As we sing red songs, our will for struggle churns the seas and makes the
  continents tremble
Knock those capitalist roaders down; throw the oppressors to the ground
  and trample them once again

05:03, November 16, 2012. Changhe-wan in Beijing.

A MONOPOLISTIC INTEREST GROUP

What was wonderful about Cult-Revo was the concerted effort people
    made to upend and smash almost anything
People wore the same clothes, sang the same songs, and drank the same red
    kombucha
Now we all talk about the socialist market economy and letting some of the
    people get bulging pockets first
They buy houses like buying cabbages, and they drink Moutai like it's water
They have plenty of money, so they farm it out at high interest, which is
    called "appreciation of state assets"
Sitting at a receipts window, their progeny need only extend their hands to
    get hundreds of thousands of RMB
To hire migrant workers, they adopt the labor dispatch system, paying only
    daily wages
Even their mistresses carry Hermes bags and drive Maseratis
They say they are the legitimate children and love children of the Republic
They see themselves as the "red generation" that can be allowed to get rich
    first
In order to hand down their wealth, they need to make sure that "the sky
    does not change color"[1]
I am one of those tycoons; my standpoint and ideas are consistent with theirs
But in red songs I hear: "wind howls, horses neigh and the Yellow River roars"
How can I not worry when banner-wielding migrants outside my building
    chant "Money for our sweat and blood!"

05:58, November 16, 2012. Changhe-wan in Beijing.

---

1. "The sky does not change color" is a metaphorical way of saying that the current framework of power, buttressed by Marxist ideology, remains intact.

THE CORRUPT ESCAPEES

On the streets of Los Angeles, I know who the escapees are
That gray-haired lady handing out leaflets in praise of Falungong[1] is doing it
    for a green card
That plainly dressed, shifty-eyed man with a lowered head was a corrupt
    official
Those grizzle-headed men who go out to buy a *Sing Tao Daily* want to know
    who has been extradited
China's concept of the "naked official" shows that the Cultural Revolution
    can happen again[2]
That is to say, an era when homes cannot be ransacked may also be a cause
    for grief
Think about it: by the time those tycoons' affairs are in total disarray, they
    have already flown the coop
They take the Republic's profits to a capitalist country, where they use the
    money to live in peaceful retirement
In fact, the red guards were clear-sighted, and their will to struggle was firm
It would take a leather belt to make today's corrupt bureaucrats into
    upstanding folk
I grieve for my motherland; I grieve for my wealth and even for my Cult-Revo
I want to stand up and pluck a tree leaf for a whistle, to play a plaintive tune
We have overthrown capitalist roaders only to foster new capitalist roaders
We provided for a generation of poor people only to let a new generation of
    poor people appear
Isn't it sad that we pulled off our armbands only to be torn by the desire to
    wear them again?
Isn't it absurd that we want to wield our fists again, as we did when we were
    red guards?
Here we can see the corruptness of history, making it forever unworthy of
    our trust

06:22, November 16, 2012. Changhe-wan in Beijing.

---

1. "Falungong" is a new religion, founded by Li Hongzhi, which is suppressed in China but has adherents in overseas Chinese communities. Some Falungong practitioners have applied for and received political asylum in the United States, on the grounds that they would be persecuted upon their return to China.
2. A "naked official" is an official who has already sent his wife and children to live overseas, so he is prepared to leave China at any time.

 AFTERWORD

Social progress in China will surely require a thorough cleansing by means of historical memory. Without mentioning other convoluted, sanguinary political struggles, at least there needs to be a reckoning about that dismal time called the Cultural Revolution. It was the Cultural Revolution that deprived our nationality of its sense of shame, sense of morality, and sense of gentility, allowing these to be replaced by a hoodlum temperament, a scoundrel mentality, and a culture of mutual condemnation.

Since World War II, Germany has been conducting judgments of its Nazi past. More than 30,000 public tribunals have thoroughly cleansed the national memory of its sins. Once a nationality feels a sense of guilt and shame, it can regain self-respect and the respect of others. As for us, we all feign forgetfulness, or perhaps we skirt this sensitive issue by stressing our orientation toward the future. A problem is thereby incurred, namely that we will have to face red guard armbands and Rebel Faction banners again someday. That would truly be a historical calamity for our people.

I was a participant in the Cultural Revolution. Because of my tender years, I did not personally take part in the carnage, but a spirit of struggle was fostered in me. Despite my cultural refinement, my mind frequently harbors murderous impulses and vile notions. Why? Because I am a red guard just as I always was. Given our present society, in which the post–red guard condition is still prevalent, it is hard for anyone to extricate himself from the struggle mentality. We are faced with a *fin-de-siècle* mentality, with rampant corruption and violent tendencies—all of which indicate that we live in a post–Cultural Revolution era. This is because we have not yet settled accounts with the Cultural Revolution, or because we think we need its continuing influence. This is our tragedy.

China's predicament of modernity was shaped in the Cultural Revolution. Vast masses of people, for the sake of "dictatorship by the proletariat," were willing to give up their freedom; for the "advantages" of armed strife, they surrendered their dignity.

Under the grand narrative of a populist movement that would sacrifice everything for national renewal and the motherland's future, our whole society plunged into ruthless—even murderous—factional strife. If we say that modernity is a time of multiplicity, we must admit that our modern predicament will surely confront us with plurality and difference. Perhaps we can still indulge in a grand narrative under which we forgo our freedom and dignity, but at some point we need to offer an explanation. Underneath this grand narrative, what is the point of our existence? Having raked in wealth during a boom phase, we cannot just go on leading a *nouveau riche* life and enjoying ourselves materially. As a nation, we need to cleanse China of its historical burdens; as individuals, we need to cleanse ourselves through repentance. Our whole nationality needs redemption from the wrongs we committed, and from wrongs we may commit again.

This was my goal in creating this collection titled *Memories of the Cultural Revolution*. Poems like these could only have been written by someone of our generation, because we were perpetrators of violence who came around to repentance. As to whether these poems partake of truth, goodness, or even beauty, those are considerations outside of the poems themselves. Together these poems constitute a story, a collection of modern folk songs, a lament, an account of nauseating memories. They can hardly be called tokens of good fortune—neither for the writer nor for the reader. In other words, we are all unfortunate.

Finally, once again let me curse what happened—in the name of poetry.

Luo Ying
July 31, 2013